MW01194164

Two Years of Trump on the Psychiatrist's Couch

David Laing Dawson MD
FRCP(C)

Edited by Marvin Ross

Text © 2018 by David Laing Dawson

All rights reserved

The use of any part of this publication reproduced, transmitted in any form or by any means mechanical, digital, photocopying, recording or otherwise, without the prior consent of the publisher is an infringement of the Copyright Laws.

Library and Archives Canada Cataloguing in Publication

Title: Two years of Trump on the psychiatrist's couch / David Laing Dawson, MD, FRCP(C).
Other titles: 2 years of Trump on the psychiatrist's couch
Names: Dawson, David Laing, 1941- author.
Description: Collection of blog posts.
Identifiers: Canadiana 20189068183 | ISBN 9781927637326 (softcover)
Subjects: LCSH: Trump, Donald, 1946-—Psychology—Blogs. | LCSH: Trump, Donald, 1946-—Mental health—
    Blogs. | LCSH: Presidents—United States—Psychology—Blogs. | LCSH: Presidents—Mental health—
    United States—Blogs. | LCSH: United States—Politics and government—2017-—Blogs. | LCSH: Dawson,
    David Laing, 1941-—Blogs. | LCGFT: Blogs.
Classification: LCC E913.3 .D39 2019 | DDC 973.933092—dc23

ISBN 978-1-927637-32-6 First Published by Bridgeross in Dundas, ON, Canada

Table of Contents

Introduction

It is perilous for a psychiatrist to write about a political figure. First it is unethical to analyze or diagnose someone without actually examining that person within the social contract of a doctor/patient relationship. And to make those findings public one needs the consent of the patient.

And our analyses, formulations or diagnoses are context dependent. That is, the purpose of these labels and interpretations is to help (alleviate suffering first) someone who is a patient.

No matter how much science lies behind these formulations and diagnoses they are still words, words that carry implications, much baggage, and interpretation is required.

Let's take the word "narcissism" for example. We all know what it means, roughly, and how it is derived from a Greek Myth of a beautiful hunter who had so much self-regard that he fell in love with his reflection in a pool and could not leave the pool. Eventually his passion for himself and his reflection consumed him and he turned into a flower.

Curiously that myth also includes devoted followers who commit suicide for him.

Of course narcissism is not a thing. It is a spectrum of implied inner traits (implied by others from observations of behaviour) of self-regard. How much is too little? How much is too much? How much is extreme? We all need a little just to get out of bed in the morning.

Within the social contract of a doctor/patient relationship, this idea of narcissism only arises when we see these implied traits limiting or hurting our patient. When they seem to be the central problem, limiting relationships, limiting vocations, causing harm to self and others, then we might add the word Narcissistic Personality Disorder.

Even then we might argue whether it is a bona fide fixed trait, or an extreme overcompensation for its opposite. And what is an appropriate (or good, functional) level of self-regard for a child, a teenager, a young person, a mature person, especially in an age of "identity politics" and "being the best self you can be."? At what point for a political leader does narcissism contribute to success, or make someone a wonderful subject for satire, or be dangerous for others?

1

And when we colloquially call someone "narcissistic" it is never meant as a compliment.

So many caveats.

But, but, we live in a moment of history when the leader of the free world (as the president of the United States is so often called) may hold in his hands the future path of democracy, the fate of millions all over the world, and, ultimately, the fate of our planet.

And that fact, I think, trumps (sorry) all the caveats. It is a time that anyone who can see the dangers posed by this man has a duty to speak up.

I started these blogs before Donald J. Trump was improbably elected. The most popular among them has been my assessment of Donald J. Trump's mental and emotional age. I arrived at an age simply from observations of his behaviour and his statements, while asking the question, "At what age in development would one expect, or not be too shocked, to observe this behaviour?" I came up with an average of 14. Though occasionally his displays of sibling rivalry and his assessment of his own greatness are definitely pre-pubescent.

We become easily inured, desensitized. The outrageous and abnormal can be made to feel normal. A step at a time. The German government enacted something like 50 laws over a short historical period, starting with restricting Jews from Union Leadership.

Some of the political pundits on television comment regularly on the "abnormal" becoming "normal". But the very presentation on TV contributes to the desensitization.

These blogs constitute my interpretation of the journey we are on with the Presidency of one Donald J. Trump as it is happening.

On Putin, Bush, Trump and the Canadian Election Session 1

September 21, 2015

We must pick our leaders wisely.

Russia currently has Mr. Putin, the Macho Man. He loves nothing more than to bare his chest, let his pectorals ripple, to hunt large animals, display his strength and resolve. He feels he embodies his country, and many of his countrymen feel the same.

This is dangerous.

Then we had George W. Bush. As I watch Donald Trump I am gaining some sympathy for George. George wasn't smart, but he tried. When he mangled our common language, when his words issued from his mouth in stumbling contradictions and malapropisms, one felt he was trying to say something intelligent and reasonable but he just didn't have the skill or the mastery of language. When he talked in black and white terms, and borrowed his language from young adult fiction ("evildoers" for example), I felt he would be more nuanced if he could. When he backed stupid policies I felt he wouldn't do this if he actually grasped the probable consequences of them. He probably did actually believe one could just invade Iraq, destabilize the Middle East and set them all on a path to democracy.

He was dangerous.

And now we have Donald Trump. His use of language is even less sophisticated than that of George W. Bush, but I get the feeling it is a pose, a performance. A performance by a very narcissistic man with no scruples. None whatsoever. Willing to play on every base fear of a semi-educated American public. Appealing to the adolescent super-hero fantasy that plays, occasionally, in everybody's mind. Willing to play on fears, prejudices, pride, and myth. I think he loves the idea of being president like he loves the idea of having his name on large impressive buildings.

The pundits don't think he can be elected. They hope he will crash and burn. But he might not.

He is very dangerous.

So (God help us) we may have Putin and Trump at their respective helms in the same decade.

This will be extremely dangerous.

If Canada is to ameliorate this danger to any degree we must have a leader who could do so. A Mike Pearson maybe. Not Mr. Harper. Mr. Harper is smarter than Trump or Bush, and more civilized than Mr. Putin, but his instinct is boldness, brashness, assertion of power and control; he would like to be emperor. He is not dangerous within our parliamentary democracy, but should he find himself sitting at a table with Trump and Putin, could he avert disaster? Or would he too thump his chest and get us all killed?

Mulcair and Trudeau have not been tested. But either of them, at that table with Trump and Putin, is more likely than Harper, I think, to suggest a peaceful solution, to negotiate, to mediate, to avert disaster, to be a second Mike Pearson.

And either would probably be better for mental health policy.

From the Twin Towers to Trump – A Canadian View of the US Session 2

January 24, 2016

There are many Americas, some of them just ideas, dreams, impressions, some of them real people living in a country bounded by Canada, Mexico and two oceans.

We were in Chantilly just north of Paris when the Twin Towers came down. We actually did witness a couple of mid eastern males celebrating as they exited a bar that night. In the morning as we put suitcases back in our rental car our innkeeper offered his sympathies. They are 'Veeruses' he said, referring to Islamists. 'Veeeruses'.

Over the next few days I found myself developing a warm place in my heart for America, the idea of America, and New York, that greatest of cities. As a Canadian I had always felt the usual Canadian ambivalence toward the U S of A, one part envy, one part disdain. But now I was suddenly American, a citizen of the new world, the place where we humans tried once again to create a vibrant, democratic, just society, a place where everybody could have a decent life, and most importantly, a place where tyrants, demigods and would be dictators could never find purchase. How dare these 13th century primitives attack my America?

Of course George Bush then invaded Iraq and I reverted to being Canadian, with less envy now, and more disdain and discouragement.

Twelve years later our news channels, talk shows, social media, magazines, and newspapers are full of Donald Trump, mass killings, the shattered politics of the USA. We see the unrest in American cities after yet another white cop shoots a black kid. We hear unfathomable, stupid opinions about gun ownership, massive armies at the ready, air power, drones, Jesus, angels, illegal immigrants and Muslims. Enormous prisons. The Failure of the mental illness treatment system. Executions. Walls being built. Trillions of debt at all levels of

5

government. Open carry and concealed carry.

From north of the border it seems as if the U S of A has become a throbbing mass of uneducated discontent teetering dangerously close to self destruction.

Yet once again we are traveling in the USA, right at this moment on I 95, moving quickly toward Sebastian Inlet State Park, and once again we have seen this country as vast and rich and busy, organized for efficiency and pleasure. As I leave the gas station store a man enters. He says, "Howya doin', Buddy?". The older black man with a worn air force baseball cap and a well groomed white poodle in the parking lot of the highway motel tells me she's a service dog. "I have PTSD", he says, "From the Viet Nam war." His candor is almost too much for my Canadian ears.

The gardens are splendid, the houses grand, and those houses that are not grand are clearly serviced and livable, the stop lights work, there is electricity available all day, drinkable water, abundant food, friendly, helpful people, black and white, selling, buying, playing with their toys, speaking their minds, driving their vehicles on well marked roads to shopping plazas to buy a vast number of products, gadgets, appliances, conveniences often invented by Americans.

Now it is true we drove past a sign on the highway stating that Georgia, to date, had 1331 traffic fatalities this year, and over 30,000 Americans kill themselves or another American with guns each year, and we are not visiting inner city Detroit.

But my point is that this vast, rich, democratic republic deserves better than Donald Trump and the rest of those republican candidates speaking in inferential half sentences and making school boy faces at one another while stoking fears of an imaginary invasion. In psychiatry this is called displacement.

Where are the Eisenhowers and Kennedys?

The world needs a just, stable, sane, thoughtful America. An inclusive America. An America that lives up to its ideals and its people. An America that can lead the world by example, not by threat.

And it needs leaders who are courageous enough to address the real needs and threats and not pander to our primitive instincts. Such real needs and threats as education, health care, income inequality, gun violence, mental illness treatment, CO2 emissions, racial and gender

6

equality – and not some mostly imaginary invasion of illegals and Islamists.

The Future of American Foreign Policy Session 3

May 30, 2016

Donald J Trump @ realDonaldTrump
Hey Justin. You go girl. Elbow those Commies. I'll cover your legal bills. I got your back.

Donald J Trump @realDonaldTrump
@JudgeGonzalesCuriel. Mexican. Hostile, hostile, a hater. Total disgrace, okay. They should look into him. This is real life folks. OK.

Donald J Trump @ realDonaldTrump
@Putin my man. Love those pecs and delts. But I got it big where it counts. Lemme tell ya. Okay.

Donald J Trump @ realDonaldTrump
@China. Yo, leader, keep your pathetic little planes away from our thunderbolts. I'll make you a deal. I'm a great deal maker. You better believe it. Got a whole University available. Good Price.

Donald J Trump @ realDonaldTrump
Really Merkel, can't you find anything classy in your closet. Come to New York and let me buy you some clothes. Not a bathing suit though, lol. Eww. Disgusting.

Donald J Trump @ realDonaldTrump
You see people. What'd I tell you. Another plane down. Pathetic. #ISIS, Al queda, whatever. You can't hide from me. Your days are numbered. I promise you. Okay.

Donald J Trump @ realDonaldTrump
@Israel@therealNetanyahu. Hey, we're behind you buddy. Send me the specs on your wall. You notice those Palestinians look like Mexicans. Eh. Huh. Huh?

Donald J Trump @ realDonaldTrump
@Vincente Fox. Funny accent man. You are a pathetic loser. I'm a winner. See next.

Donald J Trump @ realDonaldTrump
From@BARBfromKansas. You are wonderful. I want your baby.

Donald J Trump @ realDonaldTrump

#Muslim lovers. We've rounded up thousands. Who wants 'em? Trade for some Coptic Christians. Egypt huh, C'mon. #the dealmaker. We'll throw in some Mexicans.

Donald J Trump @ realDonaldTrump

I love women. I really do. I love them all over. Sorry, not now Melania. I'm working. See, she wants me. All women do. Even Megyn. Really. Okay. I've got it down there. I'm telling you.

Donald J Trump @realDonaldTrump

@Europe #bigwars. Hey, we saved your asses twice. Big time. Not gonna do it again. Not. Maybe you pay us for those first two. Or get your own nukes. Pathetic.

Donald J Trump @ realDonaldTrump

@Sadiq Khan. Why would I want to visit London? It's old and dirty. Oh yes. I forgot. I own half of it. Sell me your Mosque. I'll put up another Trump Tower. #thedealmaker

Donald J Trump @ realDonaldTrump

Huh, huh. @ISIS I told you I wouldn't tell you when or how. Gone baby, gone. All glowy like with radioactive particles now. Pretty sight. Okay.

Donald J Trump @ realDonaldTrump

Sorry about all those Roman ruins. Nobody really cared about them. Besides. I got plans. How about the Palmyra Casino? Las Vegas. #money. People. People. America first.

Donald J Trump @ realDonaldTrump

@Tehran. What can you do? The wind is the wind. Could have evacuated. I told you. Don't say I didn't warn you. Right. Am I right or am I right.

Donald J Trump @ realDonaldTrump

@Putin. #missiles. C'mon Vlad, you don't really wanna do that, do you? All over a little desert real estate? I wouldn't build a motel on any of it. Sand and stink. Oww. Really? You wanna see how big my missile is? Here's the button. Gonna do it. Gonna do it.

Donald J Trump @ realDonaldTrump

@Kim Hey. The Donald here. You got a little place for me on the coast. Next to Rodman maybe? I'm worth billions.

Donald J Trump and the Speech Patterns of 14 Year Olds Session 4

July 22, 2016

When I was 16 I bought an LP of my favourite band with money earned at a Saturday job in a Sporting Goods store. I'm sure this purchase did not have a great impact on the music industry.

Today though, the taste and preferences of the 12 to 16 year old demographic does have impact on this industry, much to my chagrin.

George W. Bush tried to speak like an adult. He tried to use big words at times, and reasonable sentence structure. He tried even though he often made a mess of it, combining two words and inventing a third, missing the negative qualifiers and thus saying the opposite of what he meant, turning verbs into nouns, nouns into verbs.

Obama speaks as an adult, his considered words and good syntax presumably reflecting the manner in which he thinks.

The latter clause is an assumption but one we make of everyone with the exception of a liar: how we speak extemporaneously, off-the-cuff, is a pretty good indication of how we think. Not necessarily the content but at least the form, the logic or lack thereof, the coherence or lack there of, the consideration or lack thereof.

I am of course getting around to Donald J Trump. And there is a connection with my music industry comments at the beginning of this essay.

When he is speaking off-the-cuff (not reading from the teleprompter) Mr. Trump speaks with the syntax, the semantics, the grammar, the choice of words, of a 14 year old. Actually when he is being positive he sounds like a 14 year old girl (randomly repeated superlatives, in random grammatical form), when negative, like a 14 year old boy (sputtered inconsiderate name calling and accusations).

The fact he speaks like this and therefore probably thinks like this is not the most puzzling fact. What is very puzzling to me is that a large American demographic now finds this acceptable, is not troubled by it, takes it in stride, even echoes it.

How did this happen? I'm sure they expected more from their presidential candidates through the last 100 years. Now, they can't all be Winston Churchill or Pierre Elliot Trudeau, able to quote scholars and parse clever phrases on the run, but at least all presidential candidates spoke an adult form of English.

This leads to the depressing thought that the 12 to 16 year old demographic is influencing our speech, and how we hear ourselves, as well as our popular music. Suddenly they are, with our new technologies, dominating, by sheer volume, our written and spoken discourse. Their careless use of language (reflecting a careless way of thinking) may be influencing the older demographic to the extent that they find nothing unsettling in the thinking and speech of Donald J Trump.

They should. I know many 14 year olds. I do not want any one of them making decisions about anything beyond which instrument to play in the school band. No matter how many adult advisors Mr. Trump gathers around him, there will come a time he is on his own. In the job of president an inconsiderate, impulsive remark, or action, can have grave consequences for us all.

I bought that LP on my lunch hour and took it back to the Sporting Goods Store. The owner asked about it. I then told him, with the enthusiasm of a teenager, that this LP featured the best band that ever recorded music. I don't remember exactly what I said. I may have used some Trump superlatives: "Big, Amazing, Wonderful". But I do remember what my adult boss said. He said, "In your... very... limited... experience."

The Thin Veneer of Civilization – Another Plea for Gun Control Session 5

July 25, 2016

It occurred to me watching the Republican Convention, the commentators who invoke Jesus and the latest cop shooting in Florida, that one of our problems is a persistent misunderstanding of human nature.

During my residency, my immediate boss, the Chief Resident, called me into his office one day to tear a strip off me, to berate me. He was a few inches shorter than I, a few pounds lighter. I was also more popular with the nurses and more likely to have influence on our ward. As he chastised me standing there I felt the Grey-Back Ape within awaken. My rat brain stirred. The image in my mind was clear. With little effort I could pick him up and throw him through the window onto the pavement two stories below.

I did restrain myself but that moment proved indelible. I am not being overly fanciful when I reference my rat brain or the Grey Back within, for it was, subjectively, a moment of being in touch with the lineage of my species, my DNA.

We were not created in God's image. We were not born pure of heart. We are not all kind and good and righteous save for the "bad guys". We are seldom entirely rational. We don't even always act in our own best interest. No. For millions of years our families and our tribes fought and killed one another for food, and land, and water, and gold, and, sometimes, once we learned to speak and write, just for the stupid ideas being promoted by a charismatic leader. (which throughout history can be summarized in two phrases: We are the chosen ones; they are not.) We also enslaved one another from time to time.

We fled central Africa and crossed the Sahara north, each defeated tribe having to move on to find another source of food and water. My

12

own tribe, not so many years ago, was pushed off the arable lands of Scotland to the inhospitable rocks and fog of the Orkney Islands, and then had to trust the hold of a wooden ship to take them around the tip of South America to a new colony on Vancouver Island where they might find water and food and shelter again, after pushing a few Indians off the better land. Apparently the Indians called my great great great Uncle "Long Gun" which left us with a few adolescent opportunities for humor but which also means, I guess, that the laws permitted open carry at the time.

In many parts of the world we are no longer small tribes warring over food, land, water rights, and women of child-bearing age. We have, with some bumpy patches, accrued over the past 1000 years or so, a veneer of civilization. And, it is just that, a veneer that thickens at a snail's pace, but can erode over night. It is a veneer based on a slowly evolved and very complex set of rules of governance, of laws and justice, of discourse, of conflict resolution, of inclusion. In this part of the world we live within a social contract very different from that of both our distant and more recent ancestors.

If we strip that veneer away I know that I will find inside myself the clansman who fought for sheep grazing pastures, the bitter Celt who was pushed off land by the Anglos, and was probably enslaved by the Romans, and ultimately the Patriarch in the jungle village fighting, and killing, for the survival of my cubs.

A year or so ago Vladimir Putin, the Alpha male in that particular jungle, roared aloud and pounded his chest. Throughout our particular jungle middle age male journalists and politicians stood up, roared aloud and pounded their chests in answer.

The fear-aggression response is close to the surface. Our veneer of civilization is thin and fragile.

We must do nothing to weaken it, for very quickly it can erode. And then the rat brain emerges and we once again live within a cycle of fear and aggression.

Inclusion, equality of income and opportunity, equality under the law, strengthens our thin layer of civility.

Donald Trump is doing his best to gouge holes in that veneer. If he succeeds the American tribe will have the Alpha Male it deserves.

But the other major threat to the American veneer of civilization is guns. The video from Miami makes that obvious. The boy or younger man is clearly impaired in some way, sitting obliviously, playing with a toy. The older man, lying in the most non-threatening posture it is possible to assume, is trying to explain the situation; the cops with weapons drawn and aimed, lurk behind poles and cars 50 feet away. The cops are in a state of arousal; they are alert, feeling threatened, fearful, and aggressive. The Grey Back Ape is stirring within each of them.

When I am pulled over for speeding I want that officer to approach my car certain, at least to a 99 per cent degree, that I will not be carrying a gun, and that I will certainly not have an automatic weapon or assault rifle. I do not want him approaching me in a fearful and hyper alert fashion. I do not want his primitive fear/aggression response triggered.

But it will be if he thinks I have a gun or even may have a gun.

So, my American friends, if you enjoy and appreciate the veneer of civilization within which you live, if you enjoy living in a land that is much safer than that of your recent ancestors, and many times safer than that of your distant ancestors, keep the guns in the stockade. By all means break then out and distribute them if you are actually invaded, but otherwise the only one in the crowd who should have a gun either concealed or open is a police officer.

Please, if everybody is carrying and a few, like Donald J Trump, are stirring up division and anger, you are risking that fragile veneer of civilization and a return to the tribal life of fear and aggression. And that, as we know, and have seen, can erupt in chaos and violence.

And then we will be saying, while watching videos of horror and killing, "They are animals!", just as we say now watching some videos from the Middle East.

14

The Unfiltered Mind of Donald Trump – A Tentative Psychiatric Evaluation Session 6

August 12, 2016

It has become a pastime for some of us, to try to understand the phenomenon of Donald Trump, and a pastime for others to try to stop him from gaining the Presidency.

There are moments, it seems, in which he simply lacks a filter. What comes to his mind is spoken. Spoken without consideration of context, of purpose, of audience, of historical and present taboos, manners, etiquette.

Everybody occasionally makes that slip. Every politician, in a lifetime of public service, makes that slip at least once, and then has to explain, and apologize, and sometimes resign.

Clinically there are people who not only never make that slip, but punish themselves for bad thoughts, or who must undo the thought through a ritual. And others who cannot enter the simplest social conversation without first rehearsing their words. This is the problem of OCD. It is a treatable condition. Would that Donald Trump had a little of this problem.

At the opposite end, clinically, are people who blurt out whatever is on their minds. Some of these have ADD. The words are said, the deed is done, before the brain can say, "Wait a minute, this might not be a good idea."

The autistic spectrum produces a problem reading social context, but usually with an accompanying anxiety that is protective. Still, some on the spectrum have rudely pointed out my double chin, asked about my age. Others can obsess and rant about a subject of no interest to the listener.

Manics, under a pressure of speech, may step close and make an inappropriate personal remark, a comment on age, breath, body odor, or sexual parts. Though usually their thoughts are elsewhere, pondering grander questions.

People with psychotic illness, struggling to create a usable mental map of the world, can sometimes spout racist theories and generalizations that make their caregivers blanch.

Well, The Donald is not manic, nor psychotic, nor autistic. He could have some ADD (attention deficit disorder). He is bored easily, easily distracted, not known to concentrate for long on any problem, uninterested in detail, and, in a sense, quite creative. He also speaks as a teenager with ADD. Seldom can he start a sentence and bring it to logical closure without an insert or two, these inserts often derailing the original intention of the sentence.

In one of his recent gaffes, he hinted that a gun owner might limit the Presidency of Hilary Clinton. It was almost possible to read his thoughts, and watch his brain struggle to forge his original thought into something appropriate for this audience.

He is speaking. He tells us if Hilary is elected she will pick Supreme Court Judges opposed to the second amendment. "No way of stopping her folks." And then he has the thought, "unless a gun owner shoots her". This thought must come out. He struggles for a split second and manages to obscure it just a little, "Although the Second Amendment people, maybe there is."

So, he has ADD.

That alone might not disqualify him from being President. Others can handle the details, keep him on schedule and on time, debrief him briefly, channel his energy and his charisma, write his speeches for him, teach him to say no comment and smile enigmatically. That is if he is smart enough and generous enough to let himself be guided.

But in the last few days he announced that Barack Hussein Obama was the founder of ISIS. He blurts this out, likes the reaction he gets, and runs with it. He does manage an explanation that Obama pulling troops out of Iraq so quickly left a vacuum that ISIS filled, then having strained his brain with someone else's more complex explanation, he jumps back to the word "founder".

Finally he relents, and tweets, "They don't get sarcasm?"

So, we have another clue to the puzzle. He is only semi-literate.

16

Calling Obama the founder of ISIS is not sarcasm. Sarcasm is saying, "That Obama, he sure made short work of ISIS." It might have required a knowing smile and an "Eh? Eh?" at the end. That would be sarcasm. I wonder if he understands irony and double entendre and tongue-in-cheek.

So with his juvenile sentence structure, his limited vocabulary, and his failure to understand sarcasm, I have to conclude he is just not very smart.

So now we have ADD, semi-literacy, and room temperature IQ.

Even then, if he were a generous soul, a selfless soul, a man of great principle with an altruistic nature, he might be okay. Forrest Gump for president.

But there is more to this man as we know. He is insufferably narcissistic. His hair, his painted tan, his constant boasting, his angry reaction to any perceived slight.

And he is more than a little sociopathic. His empathy for others is very limited. His ability to anticipate the consequences of his words and actions is limited. He does not appear to suffer any doubts, any anxiety, nor any regrets. The fault always resides with others.

So there it is. A candidate for President who is:
- Attention Deficit Disordered
- Semi-literate
- Not especially smart
- Narcissistic
- More than a little Sociopathic.

I do not want this man to have control over anything that might affect my life, my family, my city, my Province, my country, or my world.

Note: Writing the above, because I am a psychiatrist and Donald Trump is not my patient and has not given me permission – writing the above could be considered unethical. However, between a small ethical violation and the safety of the planet, the choice is simple.

Reflections on Donald Trump and Reality TV
Session 7

August 24, 2016

I apologize for writing again about Donald Trump, but what is happening in that country south of our border may be very important for all of us. Many pundits have been sharing their views, but when you are living at the time of a tipping point in human affairs it is very hard to see what is coming.

I previously commented on Trump's off-the-cuff speech pattern being akin to that of a teenager with ADD. (my apologies to all bright articulate teenagers). Well, there are two possibilities: that is his natural speech pattern and it reflects his pattern of thought or... or he is faking it. Which means he is masterfully engaging his audience in this manner because he understands the brain of those raised on Talk Radio and Duck Dynasty. I don't mean to make light of this. It is a much worse alternative to thinking he simply suffers from some ADD, both for what it says about him, and what it says about our Reality TV and Celebrity Culture.

I remember the moment Television changed democracy. Nixon vs Kennedy. Nixon did not look good on camera. At the time people speculated that FDR would not have been elected had every household owned a television. As we know either Nixon looked better on color television or his consultants taught him how to look better next time around.

Over fifty years have passed since the Nixon Kennedy debate, and since that time the makers of film, television, and other commercial interests have become much more sophisticated in the manipulation of the human mind/brain. Which boils down to tapping into our arousal systems, our reward systems, our primitive fears, anxieties, frustrations, anger, our primitive responses, our seeking of certainty and security. The digital revolution has given them amazing tools to do this. The very tools that can make information and wisdom available to all can be used to make us play video games for days on end, binge watch a cable series, and tune in for another episode of "Reality Television". We get hooked, we say. Well, yes, that is the point. A bit of fun, then mystery, then anxiety, threat, struggle, fear (albeit vicariously) then resolution and reward, repeat. Our brains love this stuff.

(McLuhan's famous dictum "the medium is the message" sounds rather quaint now.)

Donald Trump knows this. Or he is a phenomenon created by this "Reality" TV culture.

Perhaps he is a one-off, an accidental politician, a throw-back, the subject of many future dissertations subtitled, "How and why did this happen?"

Or he is a sign of the times, a man of these times, a man who understands the way entertainment can tap into the human brain and destroy the boundary between truth and fiction, the manner repetition creates reality, the manner in which simple phrases can instill anxiety, the manner in which bluster can convince, and our brains' desire to repeat that anxiety, fear, struggle, resolution, reward cycle as often and as quickly as possible.

Like the despots who managed to corrupt nascent democracies in the past Trump stirs up primitive anxiety, fear and anger and then offers us fentanyl, the quick fix. And he does this with a mastery of the new media and an accidental or calculated understanding of the brains of the fans of Reality TV.

Well, for the sake of my grandchildren I hope this is a one-off, and less to do with the impact of absorbing reality TV, entertainment, and video games with faster and faster editing taking us through that anxiety/arousal/reward cycle over and over again for many hours each day – I hope it has less to do with that and more to do with the residual racism and sexism in the American culture. The latter can be improved over time. I don't know what we do with the former.

Donald Trump, The Nature of Thought And an Appeal to American Voters Session 8

September 12, 2016

It is very difficult to pinpoint the nature of thought.

We like to believe that our cognitive processes, our internal ruminations, our ability to formulate abstractly in metaphor and in simile, our ability to induce and deduce, to follow a train of argument to a logical conclusion – we like to believe that all this is inherently human and that most of us use these abilities to modify our words and guide our behaviours.

But it is pretty clear after we have spent some time on this earth, that much thinking is a form of after-the-fact rationalization. That is we have already acted or spoken, and now we must think of ways of supporting, explaining or justifying what we just said or did or "believe". We remain, primarily, biological and social animals, responding to the dictates of our instincts and our social imperatives. And by social imperatives I mean those social initiatives and responses driven by our biology. The same biology that drove our social behaviour in the jungles, in the forests, in the deserts.

Our biological instincts and our social biology care little for truth, for compassion, for consideration, for nuance, for complexity. They care little for members of another tribe. They care little for the distant future.

We start this way as children. As children what we say and do is driven by biology and social imperative. Our behaviour as children is not driven by thought or careful formulation.

As children when we behave badly and are questioned about it we launch into the kinds of rationalizations and evasions that only a child could and might consider within the limits of his or her vocabulary.

But we progress. As teenagers we develop some basic reasoning power, some thoughtful reasoning power. This can lead to the marvelous idealism of youth, and/or stupid behaviour founded on inexperienced reasoning. (If I jump off this roof into the swimming pool there is only a 5% chance that I will kill myself or break my neck) An experienced adult would know that a 5% chance of dying is a risk only worth taking when being treated for cancer or escaping from Syria. Not so the teenager or inexperienced youth.

Some adults give extensive "thought" to actions, to words, weighing the evidence and considering the complexities and nuances.

We want our leaders to do this, our mayors, our governors, our premiers, our presidents.

For some adults "thought" is seldom more than after-the-fact rationalization.

In a previous blog I wrote that Donald Trump's speech and thought patterns are those of a 14 year-old boy or girl. I have since listened to more of his off-the-cuff palaver. Now I don't think it reaches the level of a 14 year-old still attending school. Much of it is pre-teen. Much of what he says is of the moment, an impulse, usually no more profound than "I want cookie." "I hate my sister" or "Criminals are bad people."

When questioned about any of this he remains pre-teens, child-like, simply repeating himself, or offering a contradictory statement, or switching topics and going on the offensive. I detect no thinking whatsoever.

He does have one bit of commercial sophistication, though. He knows to repeat a descriptor several times, till it replaces our thinking with an echo. As in, "She's corrupt, folks. Corrupt, corrupt, corrupt."

We are all mesmerized by this phenomenon.

But please, my American friends, if you want to continue to live at least as well as you do now, if you want a country for your children and grandchildren to inherit, please do not let this man-child take the reigns of power.

Follow Up Donald Trump and the Nature of Thought Session 9

September 14, 2016

My Monday blog may have leapt too quickly from pondering on the nature of thought to Donald Trump. Let me try to clarify.

This is a unique situation. We have a candidate for the highest office in the land who has no track record in public service, elected office or governance. We cannot look at his record of speeches, policies, and voting to make any decision about how he might continue to perform, what his core values are, how he thinks about issues both large and small. We do not have a record of principles and problem solving to consider – at least not outside his reality TV personae, and the wild west of High Finance.

We can only look at what he says and how he says it now, during this election season. As everyone points out what he says is entirely inconsistent when substantive, often outrageous, sometimes simply untrue. Only his hollow slogans are consistent: "Make America Great Again".

So we need to ask, "How does he think? Does he have a keen penetrating mind? Can he ponder the evidence, consider long term outcome, consider consequences to people other than himself? Can he dispassionately apply deductive reasoning to the questions that will confront him. Can he look beyond his very human emotional reactions to slurs, to impasses, to challenges, to disappointments and to sycophantic praise?"

Now I must admit I think we are all a little limited in this attribute. Hence the first half of Monday's missive. What usually follows the phrase "I think…" is a rationalization. Much of what we think and say is really a defense of what we did or said yesterday or of a rigid belief we happen to hold.

Seldom do any of us apply that other kind of thought to an issue: look at the evidence with an open mind, apply logic and reasoning, consider the short and long term consequences to ourselves and others, and formulate a sensitive and considerate answer.

But that is the kind of thinking I want our leaders to have, especially those who may be called upon to make momentous decisions. We can only see evidence of this through our candidates' track records or implied by their off-the-teleprompter speech.

And I see no evidence of this kind of thinking in Donald Trump's speech pattern – in his off-the-cuff speech. In fact I see only the rationalizations, evasions, repetitions, accusations, partial sentences of a 14 year old boy with ADD. (or a ten year old without ADD)

I used the pronoun 'we' in this essay though I am Canadian and do not get to vote. Like it or not we are all affected by some of the decisions made in the White House. We are all affected by how well the President of the United States comports him or herself at home and abroad.

Especially with the darkening clouds of CO_2 emissions, refugees from war and famine, and unrest from inequality and deprivation looming on the horizon. We need a President who will put some real thought into these matters, who will listen to experts, and consider the long term consequences of any decision he or she may be called to make.

We need a President who understands it is not wise to either taunt or cozy up to a bear. We need a President who knows something of the history of Walls. We need a President who relies not on economic theory but on the evidence of what has worked for all in the past in some countries and states and what is working now. We need a President who genuinely understands the increasing importance of a very good public education system. We need a President who won't bankrupt the country or blow it

The Excited States of America Session 10

September 16, 2016

I am of an age when I might sit on the back porch and grouse about the sorry state of the world. Either that or stop watching the news. Two items disturbed me last night. They were two rather inconsequential items amidst the horrors of the Fentanyl epidemic, the disaster of Aleppo, and a Canadian company selling war machines to South Sudan. But these two items spoke of a mind set more far reaching in its possibilities than the others.

The first was the CNN report of the Iranian warning to a US plane. I listened to the warning. It was standard fare. A radar ground crewman warning a war plane that it was currently in international air space but drifting toward Iranian air space and if it entered it would be "targeted". An Iranian radar guy doing his job.

But then we have Wolf Blitzer announcing in that voice of his that I suspect could not order a cup of coffee without it sounding like Armageddon is the next customer in line, and then commentary by experts and generals and an old CIA guy. Wow. I could hear the war drums, the pounding of chests, the sirens in the missile silos.

I hope this is a matter of ratings, of audience appeal, the need to grip the audience with drama and threat and suspense. I hope the American ego is not that fragile. For if it is, and if Donald is commander-in-chief, a raised middle finger could trigger a nuclear disaster.

The second item was our Peter Mansbridge interviewing a debating expert from one of our Universities. I have no doubt there is technique involved in a good debate. And I am sure technique is everything in one of those sporting debates with an audience of students and profs scoring the event.

But the examples used were clips from the Lauer interviews of Trump

24

and Clinton. The clip of Trump had him first stating a lie, then quickly following this with two simple truths, and then diverting to an attack on Obama. The expert pointed out the form of this technique and rated it a good one that she herself has used a couple of times. Start with a lie but cover it quickly with a two indisputable truths. Mansbridge did not question this.

The boundary between entertainment and reality has disintegrated. This is a candidate for President of the United States lying, not a clever sophomore convincing us that angels do dance on the head of pins. Not a reality TV show where the only stakes are ratings and advertising dollars.

I would actually like to believe that when Trump lies it is a clever strategy he is employing. Unfortunately I think it comes naturally to him, easily, just as it does to a child.

Donald Trump vs Lincoln, FDR, Eisenhower and JFK Session 11

September 23, 2016

A depressing explanation for the existence of Donald Trump as a viable candidate for a position held by Lincoln, Eisenhower, F.D. Roosevelt, and John F. Kennedy.

Disparate data supports this hypothesis:

• I have some patients, teenagers, 20 somethings, who spend almost every waking hour in front of one or two or even three screens, absorbing Youtube Videos, Reality TV shows, and gaming. Some sleep at random times, and bathroom breaks and grabbing some food from the refrigerator are minimal, random, and treated as an interruption.

• Some years ago mental health professionals were so influenced by film and television that "multiple personality disorder" migrated from being a theatrical device to a real syndrome.

• One teenager I have seen told me she did not identify as specifically male or female. And then she went on to tell me that in fact she did not identify as human.

Two hundred years ago the average person lived within and experienced reality for 99% of his or her waking hours. Perhaps he or she listened to a storyteller once per week.

Books do transport us to imaginary places populated with imaginary people, but to make a book come alive, the writing must be clear and we must use our own imagination to visualize the pirate ship, the colony on Mars, the monster in the swamp. The boundaries between literary fiction and the reader's reality remain reasonably intact at all times. At least after grade 6.

Perhaps our ancestors in the 18th and 19th century were transported to fictional experiences as often as once per week at a theater, and once per week at a church. But no more than that.

With radio in the 20th century this transportation increased, and the power of it is evident in the consequences of Orson Welles' broadcast of War of the Worlds.

Still, absorption into a fictional universe occurred, at most, and for most, a few hours per week.

Then came television, and we couch potatoes expanded that to perhaps 20 hours per week.

And now new media, smart phones, tablets, internet, plus television and film, and a whole generation has grown up with their waking hours being divided evenly between a virtual reality (fiction and spectacle and gaming), and reality, and for some the balance has made a profound tilt toward fiction and virtual reality.

So I am wondering if Donald Trump owes his current success to a demographic that can no longer make, can no longer see clearly, the distinction between entertainment and reality, between spectacle and thought, between the absence of real consequences to bad ideas and decisions in virtual reality and the tragedies that bad decisions cause in the real world.

The proposed high wall between the US and Mexico may be a specific symptom of this confluence of reality and virtual reality. In a computer game such a wall can be built quickly and easily, the cost assigned to one's opponents. It fulfills its purpose or not. It is breached or not. It can be torn down as easily as it was put up. Even if we go bankrupt and our warrior is killed, we simply push the reset button. That ain't reality.

Donald Trump is a spectacle, a fiction, a celebrity. He is entertaining. He appeals to the petulant child in all of us. We don't worry about the consequences of his leadership, his stupid statements, his endless lies, because this is just a TV show, a Youtube video, a game. He is a harmless Avatar, and a guilty pleasure. Vicariously we can be The Donald for a while, enjoying his billions, his jets, his mansions, his trophy wife, his freedom to say whatever comes to mind, his freedom from guilt, from anxiety, from empathy. We needn't think about the real consequences of his candidacy because the season isn't over yet. And it is just a game show after all.

One Last Appeal to the American Voters Session 12

September 28, 2016

In 4 years 5 of my grandchildren will be in their teens, one turning six and another will be 21. For America and the world to be in a better place 4 years from now the following spheres of American reality must improve or, at at the very least, **not get worse**:

1. gun control
2. race relations
3. access to health care
4. public education
5. access to college and universities
6. infrastructure
7. police practices re gun use
8. reliance on Prisons
9. access to mental health care
10. a pathway to citizenship for current illegal immigrants.
11. treatment and rehabilitation response to addictions.
12. the respect and trust of world leaders and the citizens of other countries.
13. Play a large and important role in all world organizations.
14. Participation in the containment and eventual elimination of ISIS/ISIL
15. Participation in the stabilization of unstable countries.
16. Help end the civil war in Syria.
17. Participation in finding solutions to current migrant/refugee problems facing much of the world.
18. the use of renewable energy sources, reduce reliance on oil and coal, or invest heavily in the development of scalable technologies for the removal of CO_2 from the atmosphere, or both.

19. income equality. Improve minimum wage. Increase tax rates and tax recovery on the wealthy, individual and corporation. Recover tax from tax havens. Close loopholes that allow avoidance by the wealthy.

20. Work with international agencies to control nuclear proliferation and ultimately reduction and elimination of nuclear weapons.

***

Non-Americans are often appalled at the grandiosity and Jingoism voiced at times by American citizens. USA, USA, USA. But the truth is the entire world needs a good and healthy and influential United States of America. We need you to live up to your ideals.

We need you to be stable, and one of the adults in the room. I doubt the world could survive four years of deteriorating alliances, economic recession, more violence, an increasing gap between the 1% and the rest, policies built on ignorance and bluster, denial of global warming, and the angry impulsive use of nuclear weapons.

So read that list again, remove a few if you would like, add a couple more, and ask yourself which candidate for president, if elected, is most likely to improve most of those issues, or, at the very least, not make matters worse, far worse.

Donald Trump's Mental and Emotional Age?
Session 13

October 17, 2016

The recent revelations about Donald Trump, especially his barging into the dressing room of pageant contestants, left me wondering about emotional and mental age; specifically, at what age in a boy's development would we find some of Trump's behaviour, if still not laudable, at least common?

1. Peeking in the dressing room to get a glimpse of girls in partial dress: **age 13 to 15**

2. Complaining that the moderators are unfair and gave Hillary more time: **6 to 12** (preteen sibling rivalry)

3. Name calling repeatedly: age **6 to 12** (the school yard taunt)

4. Use of single word hyperbole to describe something: Age **14 to 16** ("It was like horrible, horrible.")

5. Lying even when it is not necessary: **14 to 17** (Some teens get so used to shading their responses to questioning by parents that they lie even when the truth would get them kudos). Donald could have said, truthfully, that he decided, within a year or so of its onset, that the invasion of Iraq was a mistake, and he would have sounded thoughtful and mature.

6. Never taking responsibility; it is always the fault of someone else: age **10 to 15**. ("The teacher hates me, I wasn't doing nothing when...".)

7. Boasting about sexual prowess: **16-18** (Actually at that age males usually boast about sexual prowess to an audience of peers who know the story is fiction. It's more of an in-joke than a real boast. We all understand the deep level of insecurity that lies behind a real boast.)

8. Groping or kissing women without consent. Perhaps **15 to 25** but only if the young man is brain damaged, severely inebriated, or mentally handicapped.

9. Denying the obvious truth. Perhaps **13 to 16**. ("The marijuana you found in my sock drawer – it's not mine. I have no idea how it got there.")

10. Broadly lashing out at unfairness when challenged. Perhaps age **3 to 10**, and beyond that into teens when the boy has Fetal Alcohol Syndrome (FASD) or Autism Spectrum Disorder.

11. Just a few days ago, Mr. Trump said something I haven't heard since I was privy to post football game teenage drunken banter: "Look at her." he said, implying clearly that he would only consider assaulting a more attractive woman.

12. And he keeps giving us fodder to think about. The latest: "I think she's actually getting pumped up, you want to know the truth." Now beside the bizarre accusation (he's referring to Hillary) he uses one of his favourite phrases, "you want to know the truth." There are many variants to this: "To tell the truth." "I have to be honest." "If you want to know the truth." "Gotta be honest with you folks." Now these kinds of qualifiers are not limited to adolescents, but they are precisely the phrases boys between the age of 14 and 19 use just before they lie. And addicts of all ages.

Fortunately Donald Trump's candidacy is foundering on his behaviour and attitude toward women. The threat of having him in the White House is diminishing. But really, by my calculations, if Donald Trump were to be elected, we would be giving an immense amount of power to someone with the judgment and emotional age of a **7 to 15** year old boy, and not a sober, stable, empathic, conscientious 7 to 15 year old at that.

Donald Trump and the Mind of an Adolescent
Session 14

October 21, 2016

The friends and family of Donald Trump should have intervened a year ago, as I hope my friends and family will do if I ever decide to try something for which I do not have the skills, knowledge, history or temperament. He has made a fool of himself. And at some point, that is going to really hurt.

It is sadly remarkable how far he has come in this race while being a clown, shouting slogans, inanities, lies, slander, and incomprehensible half-sentences. Let us pray he inflicts no lasting damage to American democracy when he loses in November.

The third debate is being picked apart by pundits both professional and amateur. I have little to add, except ...

Once again Trump has demonstrated that he has the temperament, language skills and emotional age of a teenager.

"No one respects women more than I do." This is a particular and entirely unnecessary hyperbole one hears from adolescents. "No one likes pizza more than I do." It is, on face value, a ridiculous claim, and the kind of hyperbole that only rolls off the tongue of someone whose awareness of others (and himself) is very limited.

It is also an example of the Big Lie, when the hole is too gaping to be bridged with a small lie.

The leaders of ISIS may have fled Mosul in anticipation of the Kurdish and Iraqi forces attacking. Donald tells us MacArthur, and Patton would be embarrassed by the lack of secrecy in planning this operation. "How stupid can they be." He went on in this vein. And what I heard was the experience, the knowledge, the strategic thinking about warfare of a teenage boy. A knowledge based on movies set in the old west and before the telegraph. Electing Trump really would be giving the role of

Commander-in-Chief to an impulsive teenager who watched George C. Scott play Patton and learned all the wrong lessons.

"She's a nasty woman." Point at her, make a face of distaste. Put it on Facebook; start a, well, "nasty" rumour in High School.

Then there is blaming Hillary for not creating a tax code that could prevent him from avoiding paying taxes. That was a good one. And it did remind me of teenagers who steal. I have heard them say that it was really the store's fault for not having sufficient security. "If they leave it out like that, what do you expect?"

Deny saying what millions of people heard you say just a few days ago. Again, who but an adolescent can convince himself of this kind of revision of reality?

And finally, the horrifying statement that he may or may not accept the outcome of the election. There it is. That alone should disqualify this man from running for office in a democracy. Self aggrandizement, putting himself, and the welfare of his ego, above the democratic process, with a hint of blackmail. It is the hint of blackmail that reminded me once again of the teenage brain. "I'll only go to school if..."

That's it. No more. Let us pray Donald J. Trump slips into oblivion and we can all recover from the obsession he has created. And let us pray that democracy and civilization can survive him.

Hillary Clinton's Emails, Anthony Weiner's computer and the Orange Buffoon Session 15

November 2, 2016

The other day one of the granddaughters was looking at photos on her mother's I Phone. As children do these days, she was deftly handling the electronic device, not the least amazed at the touch screen, flipping one photo to the side to view the next. I asked her where she thought the photos went when she "slid" them to the side. Without hesitation she pointed to the side of the device as if there were a tiny drawer available. "Down there," she said.

I asked an adult the same question, and she stumbled out an answer about going back to the hard drive, but was clearly unsure what was actually happening on that little screen.

And then I watched some news reports about the Clinton emails found on Weiner's computer which may or may not be significant. CNN reported that the FBI was using some special FBI software to examine the emails, and that it could take weeks. And then people wondered how those emails could have gotten on his computer, "thousands" of them apparently. It was or may have been a laptop shared by Weiner and his then wife, Hillary's assistant.

And off we go. Listening to the panels discuss this made me think of my granddaughter's concept of those pictures sliding back into a drawer. Very few adults seem to have any real understanding of modern digital electronics.

Hillary communicated via email with her assistant daily. Having passed through a couple of servers, this digital code would arrive on whatever computer had or contained the recipient's address, account, and password. The program being used would translate this back to

34

the original English. Either Weiner and his wife shared the laptop, or he added her email account to his computer without her knowing.

Then we have the Special FBI equipment that will take weeks to sort through the emails.

Good Grief.

Type in the word "classified" and click on Search. Add a few other key words if you want.

Then quickly tell us what you find before this orange buffoon called Donald J. Trump manages to sneak past the finish line.

Adolf and Donald, the Parallels are Growing Session 16

November 4, 2016

The Weimar Republic, a new democracy, was only 14 years old when Adolf seized power and dismantled it. The republic was young; there were insufficient safeguards; and it was actually an old and ailing Paul von Hindenburg who, as president, appointed Adolf Hitler Chancellor, and then suspended many civil liberties with the Reichstag Fire Decree.

The rest unfolded quickly as we know, and cost humanity a great deal.

Adolf and Donald use(d) the same techniques: Outrageous accusations and name calling without any regard for truth. Adolf spoke of this practice long before branding experts and internet trolls discovered memes. Both men assault(ed) the rules of civil discourse, **the** civil discourse, a social contract, absolutely necessary for democracy to flourish.

Adolf was clearly the better orator, but Trump has the alt-right bloggers and internet trolls to do his work for him.

Both have the ability to tap into the infantile rage that lingers in our brains from childhood. "Things are just not fair; someone is to blame; they took away my toys; it's a disaster; they are (stealing, killing, controlling, raping, bombing) us; why can't things always go my way; lock her up."

Both men instill a terrible fear of impending doom, and then they say they have a solution. They don't specify the solution. Trump probably has no ideas beyond walls, deportation, bombs, and torture. Hitler, as we know, had in mind a **final** solution.

Neither man was/is interested in governance. Neither man had any experience in governance. None whatsoever. Each is acting out a vision of himself: – a ten foot portrait on the wall of every public building, a

36

statue in every square. Each wants to be the central character in an heroic myth.

It is easier to see why so many Germans were angry. They were living in relative poverty and disgrace following the First World War and the imposed reparations by the side that "won" that war. And the alternative to the Nazis Party was a true socialist future, possibly a communist future.

The angry alt-right Americans? Well, they are not living in poverty or disgrace, but they have been fed a diet of privilege or expected privilege for so long that it must come as a shock that to be a white, male, uneducated American no longer gives you the keys to a Harley, the open road, and the envious respect of the rest of the world. And it no longer guarantees them subservient females and black porters.

To be useful to a demagogue, anger needs a focus. We know Hitler pointed his followers toward Jews, but also Gypsies, communists, homosexuals, even the infirm and mentally ill. Donald points to Hispanics, Moslems, immigrants, "criminals". You know he wants to point at other groups as well, but in 2016, he has to use code for liberated women, African-Americans, at least until he vanquishes political correctness (as some would call it) or civilized sensitive discourse.

In the Germany of 1933 the sane but conservative members of society, the privileged, the elite, the titled, the bankers, the businessmen, the officers, allowed the rise of Hitler. They believed he would be better for them than socialism; they believed he was, for them, a useful tool. Adolf would let them keep their privilege and power, they thought.

The same is happening in the US today. Many otherwise sane conservatives, republicans, believe Donald is a safe alternative to .....to what? "Crooked" Hillary, a woman in power, the Washington Elites; higher taxes on their wealth, restrictions on gun ownership, government regulation, and, I think, a truly integrated diverse population. But Donald will not serve their interests any more than Adolf served the interests of conservative Germans.

I do not understand the rules of American democracy well enough to conjure up any predictions should Donald become president.

A terrorist attack, a mass shooting, a Russian provocation could be the equivalent of the Reichstag Fire.

It was really not difficult for Adolf to dismantle German democracy, inflame his people, build up his armed forces and start a war. Apparently being saluted by adoring crowds screaming his name, having his portrait in every public building, having absolute power over one large country was not enough for him. (The hero in myth and comic books must overcome his fear, go to war and vanquish a foe, before receiving the adulation of his people.)

We can only hope that there are sufficient safeguards built into American Democracy to prevent Donald from dismantling it. But I fear enough power resides in the office of the President of the United States of America for Donald to do great harm to humanity should he be elected.

And, even if he loses, Mr. Trump has already opened wounds that will take a long time to heal.

President Donald Trump
Session 17

November 11, 2016

Is the election of Donald Trump a sign of the human race once again slipping into a very dark and destructive period?

History tells us it is. We humans have an uncanny ability to set in motion a series of unstoppable events that lead to mass extinction and common misery on a regular basis. And then we emerge and flourish once again, and for a while we tell ourselves that this must never happen again. And then many of us forget and focus on our immediate needs, and wishes, and desires, our disappointments, our hurt and outrage.

Old instincts kick in, the ones that served us well when we lived in small villages and tribes competing for limited hunting grounds. And then it happens all over again, a series of events that leads to a mass destruction, each time a little differently, but each time unleashing immense misery upon ourselves. As human history goes, we are at the tail end of a long period of relative peace.

Is this one of those moments? A chain of events without a definitive starting point, but including the invasion of Iraq, Egypt, Turkey, ISIS, Syria, Brexit, the rise of far-right leaders and dictators and would-be dictators in Europe and Russia, and then America.

I see on my Google news today the smiling face of Kellie Leitch espousing Trumpisms, and then that of the ridiculous Don Cherry telling us those pinko left-leaning weirdo Americans are not welcome in Canada.

Here is what I hope:

I hope we can keep this regressive craziness out of Canada. Don Cherry has evolved into a buffoon entertainer. Let us leave him in that role. Kellie Leitch is a more serious threat and she has been energized by Trump's victory, so we need to be vigilant.

I think at least much of the success of Donald Trump is a backlash, or

"Whitelash". A reaction by a certain white demographic that has, for 8 years, seethed under the leadership of an African American. They were not ready for a black president, especially one so thoughtful, articulate, so obviously popular, calm, even-handed and fair. For eight years he has been an affront to their congenital views of the other race. That part is specifically, I hope, an American development, and this Trump win might energize the sane, non-racist, inclusive elements of America.

And then we have Donald. Many of the narcissistic, sociopathic charismatic leaders who have seized power in other historical moments had the same psychological profile as Donald J. Trump, but they did not grow up with his degree of luxury, and for years they harbored and nursed specific ideological and xenophobic beliefs. Donald, as far as we can tell, never served any idea beyond his own self-aggrandizement. He has really found himself in that office without any ideological baggage, nothing he fervently believes in anyway.

Perhaps his narcissism will be satiated with people, every day throughout the day, deferentially calling him Mr. President, with his photo in every public office, with sufficient moments on television and on the front page of newspapers, magazines, and being the number one search on Google – perhaps his narcissism will be sufficiently satiated so that he can quietly let other people (who may actually understand the complexities of the world and have some empathy) govern while he primps for the next photo op, and gives good speeches someone else wrote for him. He wants to be loved after all.

That is what I hope.

But I know better. A healthy narcissism is satisfied with a few positive comments about one's blog, a partner who says she loves you, the improvement in the health of one's patients, children who tell you that they want their children to know you, and a smattering of applause for a job well done.

But Donald's narcissism is not a healthy level of self-regard. Nor is it scrutinized, considered, or judged by Donald's brain.

It will not be so easily satiated. For this level of narcissism there is no endpoint, no level of stasis and balance. It requires larger and larger doses of adulation. And for this he needs to face a crisis, walk across a battlefield of dismembered bodies, make life and death decisions, stand atop the pile of misery, face increasing threat (even if of his own making) and conquer it and be rewarded with unflinching adulation and adoration.

Such hunger could lead, eventually, to his destruction, and a great deal of suffering for the rest of us.

I hope I am wrong. Perhaps having achieved far more than his father, Donald can now rest on his laurels, cocooned from his critics by White House staff, and let competent others make sensible decisions. Perhaps his pragmatism may be a bulwark against the ideologues of the Republican party. Perhaps.

On the Death of Leonard Cohen and the Election of the Donald Session 18

November 14, 2016

My son and my stepdaughter sent me condolences on the loss of Leonard Cohen. I had not realized that my life-long affection for his songs and poetry had been so obvious.

Perhaps they noticed that his lyrics were the only ones I could sing beyond the first line. Perhaps they noticed he was always playing in my studio. Perhaps they noticed I listened to little else but Leonard.

I was just recovering, somewhat, from the Donald Trump win when Google told me Leonard had died. I did not want it darker. But darker it became.

It is hard to imagine a greater contrast.

Leonard examined, struggled with, wrote songs about, all that makes us human. When he experienced desire he worried it, examined it, thought about it, considered it. His struggle to find meaning was fodder for his lyrics. His yearning and the consequences of yearning were examined with a poet's heart. He considered his fame and fortune, his loves and his losses. He considered his relationship to a possible God, or a meaningful universe. He struggled with depression and he told us about it. Through his poetry he found ways to tell us of truths, paradoxes, and of social fictions.

"There is a crack in everything. That's how the light gets in."

"Democracy is coming to the U. S. A."

"Old black Joe's still picking cotton. For your ribbons and bows."

He was earth bound but reached for the stars. "But you don't really care for music, do ya?"

His was a life examined and shared. His lyrics often surprise and they d0 let the light in. Like many songwriters he started with first love, but then he examined the rest of his life as he lived it, all the way to

42

impending death. He created fresh poetic images that linger in the mind. "Suzanne takes you down to her place by the river." "Like a bird on a wire..." "So long, Marianne.."

His voice got better with age, deeper, richer, more resonant.

Donald Trump examines little but his own image in the mirror. He recognizes no complexity to human life. He confuses love and hate. His desires go unchecked and unexamined. He pursues his yearnings without thought for the effects they might have on others.

His speech and manner are the antithesis of poetry.

I will continue to listen to Leonard. Thank you, Leonard, for all you have given us.

Unfortunately I will have to pay attention to Donald over the next four years. But when he becomes too much to bear, I will listen to Leonard.

Anxiety and the Trump Presidency Session 19

November 21, 2016

I must admit that every time I experience a small surge of optimism following the Trump win, it is quickly dashed by news of how little he understands about the job he will soon have, his indifference to the suffering of others, ("They can go to another state for an abortion"), his choice of an alt-right racist, misogynist provocateur as his advisor, and the fact that by American rules he does not **have to** distance himself from Trump Enterprises. It is a tradition, it is a necessity of democracy, but not required by law. I had assumed he would have to keep arms length at the very least.

American democracy is even more fragile than I imagined.

Now we have news that there has been an immense and sudden increase in mental health crisis calls across the United States from people who feel threatened and vulnerable.

The other day a Jewish colleague smiled. He was more relaxed now about the Trump win, he told me. Trump's son-in-law, he had heard through Jewish sources, would be playing an important role, perhaps even Chief of Staff, in Trump's white house. And this man, Jared Kushner, is sane, educated, decent and a Jew. My colleague was optimistic in a conspiratorial manner.

And I wondered at the time, I must admit, if the anxiety of the Jews of Germany had been similarly assuaged in the early 1930's.

Which leads me to three pieces of advice or caution:

All democracies are fragile. They are cultural artifacts, products of social, not biological, evolution. They can be dismantled quickly. Be vigilant. In Hitler's Germany the Jews suffered 400 incremental restrictions of their rights between 1934 and 1939, each taking away a facet of their social and personal lives until all that was left was being. And we know what happened next.

We humans are not far from the jungle. Our instincts are not

44

democratic. Nor are they primarily altruistic. We are easily led to act against our own real (long-term) interests. We absorb the fear and hate of the crowd. We can revert quickly to tribalism. We can be easily fooled. We are vulnerable to wishful thinking. Our religious books mislead us by suggesting that at the core of each and every man or woman there is a decent being. No. They also mislead us by telling us that there is a God looking after us, who has a plan. Don't be ridiculous. Inclusiveness, caring beyond family and tribe, kindness to all, empathy for all, especially caring what happens to the entire planet – these are very recent value-added human traits. They are easily stripped from us by fear and loathing, both real or imagined and/or promoted by a demagogue. Each and every one of us is capable of sinking to a level of depravity that allows us to do unthinkable things. Perhaps 5 to 10 percent will resist this until death, but another 5 to 10 percent, I'm afraid, will revel in it. The rest will continue the water boarding if ordered to do so. You know in which of these groups Donald Trump resides.

Anxiety is a response to threat, or perceived threat. It is contained or dissipates when we feel we have some control. So take whatever control you can. Join groups, join protests, write, speak, vote, participate. Be vigilant. Do not allow the first of those 400 incremental steps to the unthinkable.

p.s I wrote the above before Mike Pence attended "Hamilton". There are times in our lives when even the most self-centered and ego-threatened of us can be generous of spirit. It is easier, as we writers know, to congratulate a fellow writer on the publication of her novel if ours has been published as well. It is easier for the winner of a race to hug his opponents. If there were any time in the life of Donald J. Trump when he could afford to be generous of spirit it is now, while the triumph rings in his ears and the hard work is yet to begin. No matter how fragile his ego, this should be a time he can listen. But no. He tweets out demands for apologies and petty remarks.

Beneath that mop of blonde narcissism lies the mind of an insecure teenager.

My friends, your anxiety is justified.

Predictions for the Trump Presidency Session 20

November 24, 2016

The good news:

Donald Trump has neither the knowledge nor patience to figure out how to repeal parts of Obamacare, renegotiate NAFTA, build a great wall, prosecute Hillary, create the mechanisms to actually find and deport 3 million immigrants, or even change the tax system.

He won't interfere much with climate change accords, because he doesn't really care one way or the other and this is also a very complicated endeavor. He will continue to contradict himself from day to day, responding to his immediate impulses and his (I must admit) well honed intuitions about his public.

He can interfere with the TPP because all he has to say is, "Not gonna do it." China can take the lead and a trade deal will be struck with all countries on the Pacific excluding the USA. I have no idea what that means for the USA or Canada.

Anything that requires a great deal of work, attention to detail, building a consensus, formulating a complex plan, he will not do.

The bad news:

Within a few weeks of his presidency Donald Trump will manage to mix his business dealings, his self-aggrandizement, and his petty peeves with his presidency, with his representation of the people of the United States, to such a degree that the democrats and a few republicans will start an impeachment process. In the ensuing hearings his business dealings around the world and at home will be exposed. He will respond with anger and outrageous accusations. This will convince others to support the impeachment.

As it becomes clear that Donald J. Trump will be successfully impeached he will become a raging bull. He will not simply announce, "I am not a crook." and board the helicopter in disgrace. He will rage. He will suffer an extreme blow to his narcissism. He will rage and lash out.

This will fuel the racist fires at home and cause great anxiety abroad. He could well bring the temple down.

Sane American leaders need to be thinking about a contingency plan.

Perhaps the fully sane leaders of the rest of the world could form a club and plan a contingency of their own. What to do when King Donald goes mad.

Reflections on Democracy in the Age of Trump
Session 21

December 14, 2016

Some very smart people have been pessimistic about the staying power of democracy.

"When the people find that they can vote themselves money that will herald the end of the republic." – attributed to several American Statesmen and Politicians.

"The best argument against democracy is a five-minute conversation with the average voter." – Winston Churchill

"Democracy cannot succeed unless those who express their choice are prepared to choose wisely. The real safeguard of democracy, therefore, is education." – Franklin D. Roosevelt

"Democracy... while it lasts is more bloody than either aristocracy or monarchy. Remember, democracy never lasts long. It soon wastes, exhausts, and murders itself. There is never a democracy that did not commit suicide." – John Adams

"Democracy substitutes election by the incompetent many for appointment by the corrupt few." – George Bernard Shaw

Yet those of us born into, growing up and spending our adult lives within a democracy, assume that with every passing year it will grow stronger, more resilient, and less easy to corrupt. And that would be, I think, the consensus of academics, philosophers, political scientists: that with many safeguards in place, a separation of governance and religion, civilian control of the military, an independent judiciary, a functioning economy, literacy and education, voting rights for all, transparency and openness, a decent and wise constitution – that with these in place democracy can but flourish.

But.

A friend of mine, a fellow medical student at the time, was the son of the first minister of the crown in the British Commonwealth to be convicted of fraud. It was purported to be a $5,000 bribe he accepted from a major corporation. I remember being puzzled by the smallness of the bribe. It seemed a paltry amount upon which to risk one's career, family, reputation, livelihood. Some have whispered in that time-honoured conspiratorial manner that the $5000 was only the tip of the iceberg and what they could "get him on". But I have come to understand that our individual sense of entitlement is so strong, so close to the surface, that it can be easily manipulated by the unscrupulous, or simply by our own grandiosity and narcissism. How else can one explain our vaunted Canadian senators hedging their expense accounts? Let's face it. All it takes is a $50 gift and a letter extolling your brilliance and goodness. Just sign here.

So democracies are fragile. And not just those nascent democracies of Chile, Argentina, Brazil, Venezuela, Turkey. The old, established ones as well.

The foreboding elements are now in place: seriously unequal wealth distribution, increasing tribalism triggered by migration, mass media mechanisms for the dissemination of fake news, and, in the USA, a floundering public education system, competing religious extremes, the inevitable failure of the American Dream for the majority of Americans, a festering and historic racial divide, a warrior culture, a culture that celebrates celebrity above all else, a culture that is skeptical of experts, where many think the facts derived from science are simply opinions, a culture with rather simple notions of "good guys" and "bad guys", a manipulated information system, and the election of Donald Trump.

Americans are at risk of losing their democracy. We are all at risk of war and economic collapse. I have no idea exactly how these events might unfold but I am sure they have moved from the impossible column to the quite possible column.

As well, it seems, surveys of the populations in several democracies find a growing percentage of people who think an alternative to democracy would be okay. Close to 50 percent say they could live without it. This laissez-faire attitude is especially prevalent among the generations who have only known democracy.

There have been a few moments since the election when it seemed that maybe this will be all right, we will somehow muddle through, when Donald is reported to have said something sensible, conciliatory, inclusive. But, for the most part he remains Donald Trump, and my fears are growing.

I won't go over all that he has said and tweeted, the inordinate amount of time he has spent focused on petty grievances, watching SNL, celebrating his victory – or on his sketchy appointments, his lack of attendance at briefing sessions, his poking a stick at China and at the findings of his own CIA. But I would like to point out a few things he has said, and the way he has said them. For they are more telling. They are more telling about his level of narcissism, his tone-deafness, his lack of knowledge, and his grandiosity.

At a rally after congratulating himself on being named person of the year by Time Magazine, he commented to the crowd that maybe the title should be returned to "**Man** of the Year". Eh? Eh? Apparently the crowd cheered.

When asked why he didn't attend intelligence briefings, he answered, "I am, **like**, a very smart person."

When being asked about answering the call from Taiwan, and then questioning why we have a one China policy, he said, "I won't let China push **me** around."

His ignorance is palpable even when he remembers a few catch phrases from a briefing by his people. But in theory he could learn. What is more frightening is the level of his narcissism and grandiosity revealed in those three quotations. This is a Shakespearean level of grandiosity and narcissism, the kind that leads a man to listen only to sycophants, to govern according to his own pleasure, according to his own ego gratification, and to bring the temple crashing down, to lay waste to his nation before accepting any slight, any blow to his over-inflated but fragile sense of self.

I'm afraid I only see three possibilities. The electoral college votes against Trump, precipitates a constitutional crisis, and stokes the American divide, or he is inaugurated, and then impeached, precipitating a constitutional crisis and stoking the American divide, or we all spend the next four years on the brink of nuclear war while watching regressive policies being put in place.

Trump and the Women's March Session 22

January 23, 2017

Sitting in the lounge of the Vancouver airport waiting on a flight to Edmonton I can see the snowy peaks of the North Shore Mountains lit up by the late afternoon sun. With closed caption description the large television is showing the inauguration parade, the slowed and often paused procession of a large black limousine surrounded by dozens of secret service agents.

A young woman is pumping milk from her breasts to a bottle under her shirt. I wonder where her baby is. Perhaps with her parents in Edmonton. A tall black man walks by, ear buds, furry boots, and dreadlocks. The faces around me are varied. One I think is Japanese, another appears first nations, two more are Chinese, then Korean, and then an Hispanic couple. A Malaysian man is sleeping, a white woman eating a salad from a plastic container. Many are bent over phones and laptops. Two Asian boys speak Mandarin to their mother. Her legs are slightly bowed as an older woman's might be from a deficiency in Vitamin D experienced as a child. A plump white woman walks by in slightly ridiculous brilliant red spike heels.

Trump's inauguration speech is isolationist, a warning to others. He talks of ending crime in the cities by expanding police forces, of wiping out ISIS once and for all. He speaks of desolation and destruction in America, of violence and death in the inner cities. He uses the word "carnage". He speaks of building the armed forces and respecting the police. He talks of America first, of placing a high tariff on items built by American firms in other countries. He speaks of the American education system and suggests it is rich but wasteful, a failure. He paints a bleak picture of America and hints at a law and order solution.

Our flight is late. The plane has come from San Francisco where it was delayed.

Once we are in the plane and seated with baggage stowed the flight attendant tells us the crew can manage communication in English,

51

French, Cantonese, Mandarin, Japanese, and Korean.

Trump's speech is that of a strong man, an autocrat. He doesn't name an enemy apart from ISIS and previous administrations but his code words hint at a few. He will dismantle industry regulation and Obama Care. He appeals to patriotism, power and domination.

When our plane arrives in Edmonton the attendant asks all passengers to remain seated so a man from the rear of the plane can disembark first to make a tight connection. A minute later a worried Asian man hurries down the aisle. A tall white woman gives him an encouraging smile.

It is still and cold this morning in Edmonton, the ground snow covered, the air dense with ice crystal fog. I see on the CBC news network that a similar fog has settled on Washington, though judging by the dress of the half million marchers it is warmer.

We watch the CBC coverage of the gatherings in many cities. We chuckle at the more clever protest signs: "We shall not overcomb", and a uterus with fallopian tubes in the shape of a raised middle finger.

And then I experience a brief surge of optimism. Perhaps the election of Donald Trump is but a catalyst, a shock, a wake-up call that will energize a counter evolution propelling us along the better pathway of inclusiveness, women's rights and equality, cooperation, kindness, good social programs....

The very fact there are marches taking place in many cities around the world is evidence that isolationism is impractical.

But I also see that Iran has already warned that it can easily restart it's nuclear program, and Trump is already signing some regressive policies into law.

In Edmonton we are visiting our son and daughter-in-law and their three children, all girls. I pray for their sake my optimism holds.

Trump and the Threat to Democracy Session 23

January 30, 2017

My optimism was short lived. After watching Trump's speech at the CIA headquarters and Sean Spicer's first press conference I wondered how one goes about dismantling a democracy. I assume there is no manual for this. So I thought I would create a Coles Notes version so we can all follow along:

1. Make frequent reference to the utter failure of all previous administrations. Take credit for anything good that happened during the most recent administration.

2. Promote a cult of personality. Suggest the new leader has God-like powers, such as controlling the rain, and solving complex and intractable problems with forceful statements.

3. Paint a bleak picture of the current state of affairs and grossly exaggerate the risk, the dangers posed by outsiders and nonbelievers.

4. Promote law and order and military power as the only forces that can keep us safe.

5. Incrementally reduce voting rights by insisting on regulations that favor your supporters and disenfranchise others. Do this by claiming you are controlling corruption and fraud.

6. Choose an enemy or two, give them names, and promise to eradicate them. Use emotionally inspiring words such as evil, kill, wipe them out, get rid of them once and for all.

7. Exaggerate the size of your support and the crowds attending your rallies. Refer to this as a movement.

8. Lie frequently and often. Use big, bold lies. This is a form of desensitization. More and more will believe your lies. The remaining citizens will stop caring.

9. Undermine the Fourth Estate. Seed distrust of news and information. Call all reporters and truth tellers liars. It will be difficult to fully control the media (this is not Russia) but consider using licensing bodies, libel laws and the courts to tie their hands.

10. Promote the idea that the people of your nation, your followers, are superior human beings, exceptional, and deserve to live better than others. American Exceptionalism. Or is that "Uber Alles"?

11. You will need the armed forces and intelligence agencies so flatter them frequently, while you replace their leaders with your own men.

12. You will need cabinet members and spokespeople who will unabashedly promote you and your statements and policies no matter how unpalatable or ludicrous they become. Some will be willing to do this for money, others for power and glory of their own, and others because of their own anger and resentment from earlier grievances. Unfortunately such people abound. But remember, it is not loyalty that binds them to you, but self-interest. Reward them generously; always be prepared to kill them.

13. Quickly disparage and render impotent any leader who opposes you. Memorable name calling and disinformation will suffice.

14. Create a language of code words for anything that remains unacceptable for most citizens. For example: "alternative facts" for lies, "violence in the inner cities" for racial profiling.

15. Use hyperbole at all times. A person or event is either "great", "fantastic", "amazing", or "a disaster", "evil", "total failure". This fosters a dichotomous view of the world and will help dehumanize victims when the time comes to purge.

16. Find some allies in other countries by directly or tacitly supporting their extreme views. Examples might include Putin, Duterte, Boris Johnson, Marie Penn and Netanyahu. Be unpredictable for the others. Keep them on edge.

17. Finally, incrementally increase your power and authority until you can accurately call yourself "president-for-life" or "Supreme Leader". This will take time. At some point you will need a crisis at home (Terrorist attack for e.g.) or you will need to provoke a crisis abroad and at home (Palestinian response to moving embassy to Jerusalem for e.g.). This will justify your transfer of a specific power from a democratic body (congress/senate/parliament) to your own office. This can be done on the grounds that only you know all the facts, and quick decisions are required. It is also more acceptable if the democratic bodies are perceived as ineffective or too partisan. Your people can

ensure the latter condition is met.

18. In the meantime cater to the dominant political force in the democratic body by quickly implementing all their pet projects (e.g anti-abortion legislation), and by cancelling all the social and health initiatives of that upstart negro president.

19. Build monuments to yourself. Oops. I forgot. You already have. Good. Build more. Start with the Trump Great Southern Wall.

20. Throughout this process continue to emphasize that you are working for the people. Use the words "people", "working people" and "democracy" frequently. As you usurp power explain that you are protecting democracy.

21. Have patience. Others may deliver you the crisis and fear that will allow an incremental or bold increase in power. When you assume new powers present yourself as reluctant to do so.

22. Use as much pomp and circumstance as possible. People love ceremonies. Emphasize the sacred trust your office embodies.

23. Visit a religious leader (televised of course). Ensure him and the American Public that you understand the enormity of your office and the need for God's guidance. Try not to sneer or chuckle doing this. It is not wise to compare yourself to God, but you can hint that He favors you in some way.

24. Don't worry about the physical quirks the cartoonists seize upon, the little black mustache for example, or the blonde comb over. Ultimately these will confer upon you icon status.

25. There will be protests and marches against you. Be gracious in your response to those that remain peaceful. Come down very hard on those that become violent. Emphasize these, and use them to accrue more power. But, be assured that any large gathering of people can become violent with a little help from your friends.

26. Toady up to the leaders of organized religion, the church. With few exceptions these religious leaders will see you as a means of helping them achieve their long term goals. They will not stand against you for fear of losing their own power.

27. Allow others to live vicariously through you. This is a fine balance. While allowing the people to view your sumptuous life style use colloquial language, talk as they do. Remind them you work tirelessly for them. Pretend that one day they can all live as you do.

28. Women are tricky. Have one or two around you but not many. They tend to have empathy for others, children, small animals. They tend to prefer compromise and cooperation. Reference your own dear mother frequently, and say how much you respect women. But subtly denigrate them by your own actions, and limit their voices and rights through reproductive and child-care legislation.

29. Gain increasing control of your population. You can start this by controlling all immigration and visitation to your country. Then pick the minority group most feared or misunderstood by your followers and order a registration process. This will appear harmless, like getting a driver's license. Then incrementally increase the strength of this process, include more identifiable groupings, until all citizens must carry "papers" with them and submit to police checks. This will instill fear.

·······················

But Donald Trump's performance at CIA headquarters was not so much of a man seeking autocratic rule but of unbridled narcissism. A narcissism that cannot be sated. Even a hint that the adoring crowd was not as big as Obama's set him off on a delusional reconstruction, or, as Conway called it, "alternative facts".

And his claim that 3 million votes were cast fraudulently may not be (by Donald himself) a clever ploy to undermine democracy but rather his narcissistic rage against a perceived slight. (Overall more people liked Hillary).

So I suspect he is not so much a would-be tyrant as a man needing constant adulation, threatened by any possibility he is not loved and admired as much as he feels he deserves.

But let me be clinical for a moment. In psychiatry we talk of "personality disorders" – dependent, borderline, narcissistic, sociopathic for example. Now we all have some of these traits. Who isn't a little narcissistic? But what makes a human trait a "disorder" lies in its insatiability. A dependent person can find someone to take care of him or her and life goes on smoothly. Each satisfies the needs of the other. But for some the dependency must be re-enacted and reconstructed, reinforced in each and every encounter. Then we have a problem. A little normal/average narcissism can be satisfied by a simple comment perhaps once per week: "You look really good in that dress".

But it is a disorder when it must be reenacted and satisfied in each and every encounter. When it cannot be even temporarily sated. For most of us, being elected president would suffice, or even being treated well by a store clerk.

So Donald Trump's narcissism is pathological, insatiable, needing to be reenacted, reinforced every day. He cannot tolerate even the smallest insult to his ego. This is a disorder. And such a disorder seldom ends well. In this case it could end badly for all of us.

And this flaw makes Trump an easy stooge for others who truly hunger for power and world domination. He is a blunt instrument with no guidance system of his own. I'm sure many in the Republican party are using him now, perhaps Putin as well, each hoping they can rid themselves of Donald J. Trump when their goals are achieved. Some of those goals are ideological, some are about power, some about money. But it is a high stakes game they are playing.

Please, when he has done all you desire and becomes uncontrollable, when you decide to impeach him, first take away the nuclear codes.

Quebec City – On You Trump Session 24

February 1, 2017

Mr. Trump, this is on you.

Every country in the world has a few young men capable of committing a mass murder. They are angry; they blame others for their failures; they nurse grudges; they are easily caught up in conspiracies; they rebel against any authority; they lap up the hatred of others; they spend much of their time lamenting about the state of the world while drinking beer or snorting cocaine late into the night; they are unsuccessful with women. They deeply fear the world of adult responsibility. They play first person shooter video games. They like guns. They harbor racist grievances. Some are "loners" as the newspaper will call them, but this usually means a mental disorder that limits their ability to engage face to face with others, and allows them to build a delusional world view from other sources. Of course the impersonal sources from which they can build that distorted world view, and their place in it, has dramatically increased in the last 20 years.

But usually these young men hurt few but themselves and their families. They don't (usually) act upon their darkest fantasies.

Unless they are given license to do so by someone with a loud voice. That would be you Mr. Trump. Your careless words, your disdain can unleash such horrors no matter that it was not your intention.

When I write my blogs about American politics my daughter reminds me I am Canadian. But we breathe the same air; your messages are clearly heard north of the 49th parallel. It is a sad thing the first young man who took your words and actions as license to kill was a Canadian. I trust our response to this will continue to be very Canadian.

But beware, Mr. Trump, you and Mr. Bannon have the capacity to unleash the contemporary equivalent of Krystallnacht.

When is it Too Late? Time For a Coalition! Session 25

February 3, 2017

We talk about him incessantly. We worry; we laugh; we snicker, we cry. Every day we see his narcissism on display. Everyday we see him manipulated by a handful of petty tyrants. Everyday he displays his ignorance anew. Everyday we get to see his carelessness.

And I start to wonder. When did it become too late to stop Hitler? When did it become too late to stop the First World War? When did it become too late to stop Franco, Mussolini, Stalin, Idi Amin, Pol Pot? When did it become too late to stop the Great Depression, the war in Iraq, the rise of ISIS?

Things are moving quickly my American friends. Please get together, form a coalition, if necessary put your political careers at risk, but start your filibusters, begin the impeachment process now.

I don't want my grandchildren living on a broken planet wondering when it became too late to stop Donald Trump and Mr. Bannon.

Trump's grandiosity
Session 26

February 9, 2017

I have been watching too much CNN. I must control this new addiction. It is bad enough to find oneself compelled to watch a train wreck or a car accident, to have to slow down and gawk, but now I'm following the ambulances into the ER and waiting to hear the pronouncements of the doctors and nurses and next of kin.

Each evening several panels comprised of both political persuasions dissect the president's tweets and statements, seeking substance, direction, and meaning, seeking precedent for his personal attacks, sometimes deftly skipping past his actual words to re-frame and reword the proclamation in question. They are often concerned about the political advantage or disadvantage his words might have. As George Orwell and Mark Twain and others have told us, when the outrageous lie becomes commonplace it loses its ability to outrage us. It becomes "strong opinion". It may even become "alternative fact".

But none of these panelists seem to pay attention to a part of Donald Trump's speech that I think they should. Perhaps they need a linguist on one of their panels. Like a child Trump calls the judge a "so-called judge"; like an envious teenager he revels in the low ratings of Arnold Schwartzenegger; he demonstrates every day he has no boundaries, personal, professional, or ethical.

But this is the kind of sentence I find most frightening:

"I comprehend very well, better than I think almost anybody."

Without irony or a wink he begins to tell us that he comprehends better than anybody, that he is smarter than everybody else. Then as he is forming the words he catches a glimpse of how this will sound to others, and he squeezes in the phrase, "I think almost".

He did the same when he said, "I am very smart." He squeezed in the word "like" to soften the statement a tad, even if it ended up sounding adolescent.

I can analyze this as a grandiosity that is really an over-compensation for insecurity, but it is, nonetheless, grandiosity: A belief in his own powers, in this case his intellectual powers, that far exceeds reality.

As President Kirkman said last season: "There is nothing more dangerous than a pawn that thinks it's a queen."

It is this grandiosity that will bring down the house, or some day implode in rage.

Time, Gentlemen, Time
Session 27

February 20, 2017

Open letter to all the sane and sensible Republican lawmakers who wish to see their children and grandchildren grow up in a safe world.

It is time to huddle with sane and sensible Democrats and figure out how to remove Donald Trump from office. Perhaps you are doing that already. God speed.

Thursday this past week, for almost 90 minutes, Donald Trump gave us what has been called "vintage Trump."

And in that almost 90 minutes, once again, Mr. Trump demonstrated that you have elected for your president a man who is:

- A world-class narcissist
- A man with a very short attention span (unless he is the subject of praise, and adulation)
- A careless liar. A very careless liar. *"You look at what's happening last night in Sweden."*
- A man with a teenager's vocabulary and the conceptual abilities of a 14 year old.
- A man for whom everything (and I mean everything) is about his own greatness.
- A man with very poor impulse control.
- A man with a level of knowledge of the world equivalent to that of a bright 12 year old from a good public school: *"I've been briefed…and I can tell you one thing about a briefing that we're allowed to say …because anybody who ever read the most basic book can say it…nuclear holocaust would be like no other."*
- A man with no sense of the complexities (and safeguards) of governance in a democratic system. *"The FAKE NEWS media (failing @nytimes, @NBCNews, @ABC, @CBS, @CNN) is not my enemy, it is the enemy of the American People!"*
- A man who, strikingly, does not notice, does not seem to

62

understand or care about, the meaning and inferences of his own words. *"You will never meet a person less anti-Semitic (less racist) than I am." "I'm not calling it fake news anymore, I'm calling it very fake news."*

- A man who always blames others, who cannot take responsibility for any failures or mistakes or even oversights. *"I was given that information. I don't know. I was just given it. We had a very, very big margin."*
- A man still obsessing about the woman (Hillary) who almost beat him, and the black man more loved than he.
- A man who lives for adulation, excitement, winning, not working, not actually doing a job. Hence the constant replay of the November election, and the reprise in Florida last Saturday evening.

Dr. Francis rightly points out that we should not diagnose from a distance, and that a criterion for the diagnosis of narcissistic personality disorder is that the patient be suffering, not merely wreaking havoc on others.

On the other hand, Typhoid Mary was healthy, yet few would disagree with removing her from the kitchen.

And we have lately seen glimmers of the rage within, the rage that will be unleashed when he is cornered, trapped, and finally undone.

Please read my manual for undermining democracy and note the progress to date.

"Last Night in Sweden"
Session 28

February 22, 2017

Donald Trump's reference to Sweden at his rally in Florida has been met with much astonishment and satire. He has tried to explain that he meant to reference more of a trend of refugee crime in Sweden than a single recent event. His supporters repeat this. His detractors roll their eyes.

But what he actually said and how he said it and the manner in which he absorbed the source material are, as usual, very telling. They speak to his attention span, how he is influenced, how he formulates thoughts, his limited vocabulary, and the superficiality of his cognitive processes. Here is his statement: "..you look at what's happening last night in Sweden. Sweden, who would believe this? Sweden. They took in large numbers. They're having problems like they never thought possible."

The source of this remark is a Fox News report he watched the night before. Hence the "last night". His thinking process collapses the time he watched the report and the time of supposed "events." The television screen that he watched was split screen. On the viewer's left a talking head reports an immigrant inspired crime wave in Sweden. This information was apparently gleaned from particular face book rants. But on the right half of the screen we watch videos of unidentified violence and crime: fires, vandalism, assault, riots.

The spoken information is not sourced from government data or first hand reporting but from Facebook tirades and a filmmaker with an agenda. The visual information (always more potent than words as we know) is of unknown origin and time frame.

This makes an impression on Donald Trump. He says, "You look at what's happening...who would believe this?" So he has not taken in words and images and formulated and judged them, thought about them, considered them, reflected on their meaning – no, instead he simply excitedly points to them, "You look..."

"They took in large numbers." He conjures an image of swarms of refugees rather than any considered look at numbers, programs, origins, and the problems of integration and settling.

And then, using a kind of vague hyperbole, "They're having problems like they never thought possible."

Trump frequently falls back on these kinds of qualifiers and exaggerations. They create an emotional impression without any kind of actual description, identification, or assessment. His favorites are: "You wouldn't believe." "Unbelievable" "Like they never thought possible." "Like you never thought possible."

Of course I may be wrong. Such speech patterns may not reflect the patterns of his thought; they may not indicate he has the cognitive processes of an excited 14 year old. Perhaps it is an act, a ploy, a strategy. Perhaps in private he can think and talk as a responsible adult.

Now that is a really frightening thought.

Education – More Important Than Ever
Session 29

February 27, 2017

Truly excellent, really well funded Public Schools are the answer to many of our problems and especially so in the United States. But, despite that, the US Congress has proposed a new bill (HR 610) that will gut their educational system.

Some years ago a book of essays by Robert Fulghum was published with the title "All I really need to know I learned in kindergarten". Hold hands when you cross the street. Share, be kind to one another, clean up after yourself.... It is cute and fanciful but beneath the smile of recognition there lies a profound truth.

Schools have two jobs. **Educating** our children may actually be secondary to **socializing** our children. Originally I suppose, as some sociologists point out, the goal of our newly invented schools was to prepare our children for the factory jobs generated by the industrial revolution. Show up on time, do as you are told, work all day until the Bell rings.

Many years have passed. Our schools have gone through many evolutions keeping up with the changing needs (and fads) of the times. The curricula have changed, and many of the social rules have changed, each accompanied by much dissent and discord.

But I would argue that as our cultures have become so diverse and complex, as our populations become less and less homogeneous, and as future employment becomes both less certain and more multifarious, the role of socializing our children in good public schools becomes more important. Dramatically more important.

Every kid should be sitting in a classroom, playing in the school yard, singing in the choir with at least 50 percent of the other kids being, well, different. Our children need to work with, and play with kids unlike themselves during those 12 or so formative years. Smart kids, not so smart kids, shy kids, obnoxious kids, athletic kids and handicapped kids, black, brown,yellow, white kids, poor kids and not so poor kids, kids with two parents and kids with one, kids who speak other languages, take different religious holidays, wear some different clothing.

There has of late been a rise in "hate crimes" and racial vandalism.

In a way hate crimes and racism are pernicious extremes of tribalism, and they rise in frequency when tribalism grows and especially when our leaders fan the embers.

I think to combat this we must first accept the fact that tribalism is in our genes. We are programmed to notice if someone is not of our tribe. It would be a very important trait in our prehistoric period. Science tells us that when we encounter a stranger, we first notice his dress, and then we notice his tribal markings (think hair/tatoos/metal piercings), then we pay attention to language and voice, and lastly skin colour (when we primates first developed these perceptual skills, we were likely all the same colour).

Our sense of tribe can expand, and one day might include all who live on our earth. A large swath of the white American tribe recently accepted a black man and elevated him to their highest office. Though clearly there were many who never accepted him as one of them.

Still more recently we have seen how easily tribalism can be provoked and inflamed. Brexit, Marine le Pen, Trump. We can struggle against this, we can do our best to fight this trend, but the long term solution is having every one of our children attend, from JK to 12, a well funded Public School, and a school with the complete mix of kids I mentioned before. I would allow home schooling only if, for health reasons, attendance was not possible.

I suppose I would not oppose a small number of private schools because to do so would limit some important freedoms.

I think we already see in some idealistic young people who have grown up in very diverse and inclusive schools a sense of tribalism expanded to include the whole world.

Americans especially: Do not undermine your public school system. Fund it, grow it, improve it. There in lies the hope for your future.

67

We are Now in Big Trouble Session 30

March 8, 2017

The other evening Mr. Tapper of CNN came out directly and asked the following question: Does Mr. Trump know the difference between the truth and a lie? Does he say these things as strategic gambits, all the while knowing they are falsehoods, in some cases outrageous falsehoods, or is he incapable of knowing the difference? This dichotomy suggests either he lies nastily and without regard for any semblance of truth as a political strategy, a gimmick, a distraction, or he is incapacitated.

Neither answer is very reassuring. And if this is an incapacity what is the nature of it?

There is a simple and consistent answer to this question. Pathological narcissism.

Trump's lies are responses to that which his inflated ego cannot accept. All information, evidence, facts that suggest Trump is not supreme, the best, the most popular is unacceptable to him and therefore must be denied or rebuffed with "alternative facts". Any successes or glory he does achieve must be revisited, replayed, exaggerated over and over again.

The fact Donald Trump's narcissism is extreme enough to require this level of denial of reality (the size of the crowds, the "3 – 5 million illegal votes", murder rate, wire taps) means it is incapacitating. He is incapacitated.

His lies, his tweets, are not even bounded by plausibility. They will continue, grow more outrageous, and dissolve in a wild lashing out.

Unfortunately Kim Jong Un and the excited commentary on American television may be providing Mr. Trump a way to lash out and destroy. And then, which I am sure aligns with an image in his head, he can stand akimbo in his great black coat upon the scorched battlefield like a Vulcan God.

Please, America, Please
Session 31

March 20, 2017

I have always looked to our south, like many Canadians, with a little disdain, a smidgen of envy, a touch of awe, and no small sense of superiority. When you repeat over and over again, ad nauseum, that America is the Greatest country on earth, I want to politely shout, "No, you are not." Perhaps by one measure out of twenty you are, but that's it. One out of twenty. Maybe two. Military force and entertainment. Maybe three: military force, entertainment, and some of the sciences.

You got the atomic bomb first, with the help of a few imported scientists, but Canada was second in having the knowledge and technology to build one, and it did not. Perhaps this was a much more significant accomplishment.

You can see our relationship has been complicated.

Traveling in Europe we quickly identify ourselves as Canadian, not American. I know some Americans who do as well.

But I was in Paris when the twin towers came down, and we spent four days there watching the news. And I found, out on the street, that suddenly I too was American, North American.

How dare these primitives, these semi-civilized thirteenth century people, attack the greatest city on earth, the showpiece of my America? How dare such primitives, such pre-enlightenment Neanderthals attack this beacon of light, this democracy, our democracy?

At that moment the civilized enlightened world was with you, America. You had a free hand to go hard after Osama Bin Laden. Instead you invaded Iraq. And as the war drums grew I found myself saying, "No. They won't do that. Nobody could be that stupid."

But you were. And then you did it badly, ignoring history and everything we know about collective human behaviour, about what happens when you take away stability, structure, organization.

And once again I became a disdainful Canadian watching you torture yourselves (and others).

Of course, with your own disdain of regulations and oversight, you also allowed a financial crisis to assail the world, and for the gap in wealth to grow to outrageous proportions. The very rich got richer, the poor got poorer.

And then we had 8 years of Obama, a man who proved to be, if a little indecisive, at least sane, intelligent, kind, thoughtful, knowledgeable and responsible. It looked like America had a chance again and might one-day regain a fourth or even fifth category of greatness.

Four or five out of twenty wouldn't be all that bad. Education? Health care? Quality of Life? Women's rights? Racial equality? Literacy? Scientific literacy? Standard of living? Clean air? Clean water? Mental health care? Less primitive corrections system? Modern transportation system? Banking regulations? Maybe you would even direct that famous American energy and ingenuity toward preventing the calamity of climate change?

But no.

Instead you took a mighty step backwards. You elected a child as president and a raft of 19th century idealogues to Congress. The arguments I hear on CNN about that whole list one paragraph above are silly, stupid, primitive, ill informed. With each of them the push is backwards: women's rights, health care, EPA, great lakes, mental health care, climate change, education, science, corrections, regulations, wealth equality, race relations.

Please, America, Please. Those of you who are enlightened, educated, worldly, kind, sane, responsible – those of you who have empathy for others, who have outgrown or at least come to terms with your past – those of you who care about the real future – the future for yourselves, your children, your grandchildren, and the rest of the world for that matter – you need to resist; you need to turn the tables.

I could simply go on feeling superior and disdainful, but America is too important, even the idea of America is too important. We, the whole world, need a sane, stable, educated, advanced, involved, compassionate America.

And now I shall watch CNN again and cross my fingers.

70

Trump Speak Session 32

March 22, 2017

The collection of laughable, inane, grossly inaccurate, and stupid things that Donald Trump says grows by the week. They have become the fodder of late night talk shows and the target of journalists' disdain. Satirists don't have to satirize; they merely repeat what he says.

On the internet one can also find several collections of odd, funny, nonsensical things that came out of George W. Bush's mouth. George occasionally mangled syntax; he created the odd neologism, mixing two words to make a third; he put his adjectives in the wrong place; he stumbled over language and grammar. One could make the case that he is a little dyslexic, or simply not gifted in the spoken language department.

He was on the Ellen DeGeneres show recently and he said, "...I'm going to use a big word now – symbiotic..." Ellen said, "Wow, four syllables.." The audience laughed, George smiled. And I rather liked him for a moment.

These days the journalists, the pundits, the comedians, the talk show hosts, pounce on the words of Donald J. Trump and point out their inanity, their inaccuracies, their wrongheadedness, and their untruthfulness. But beyond what he says and tweets, a true revelation of the depth of trouble we are in can be found in the way he says what he says. That is, not so much in the simple meaning to be found in his tweets and statements but the meaning hidden in the structure and form of his sentences (or lack thereof).

Whatever the subject, the reference point is himself. Whatever the subject, no matter the population actually affected, how it affects Donald is supreme. Whatever the subject, his words imply that he is supreme; they always imply that he is supreme.

Below is a list of things Donald J. Trump has tweeted or said. Let me point out what is happening in the first two. These two statements followed briefings by experts on the two subjects at hand. In them Trump indirectly admits that perhaps he didn't fully understand the

71

complex subject before, but then he quickly points out that "nobody" does. He has to say this to retain the fiction in his own mind that he is brilliant, superior, supreme, that he knows all there is to know, and all that anybody can know.

This is a very dangerous level of narcissism.

"It's an unbelievably complex subject, **nobody** knew that health care could be so complicated." (Health Care Policy)

"It's a very complex subject. I'm not sure **anybody** is ever going to really know." (climate change)

"I *know words*; I have the best *words*."

"I will build a great wall — and nobody builds walls better than me, believe me –and I'll build them very inexpensively. I will build a great, great wall on our southern border"

"I've never had any trouble in bed, but if I'd had affairs with half the starlets and female athletes the newspapers linked me with, I'd have no time to breathe."

"I love the poorly educated."

"He was a war hero because he was captured. I like people who weren't captured."

"All of the women on The Apprentice flirted with me – consciously or unconsciously. That's to be expected."

"I am totally in favor of vaccines. But I want smaller doses over a longer period of time."

"Sorry losers and haters, but my I.Q. is one of the highest -and you all know it! Please don't feel so stupid or insecure, it's not your fault."

"Cher is somewhat of a loser. She's lonely. She's unhappy. She's very miserable. And her sound-enhanced and computer-enhanced music doesn't do it for me."

When was the last time anybody saw us beating, let's say China, in a trade deal? I beat China all the time. All the time."

"I think the only difference between me and the other candidates is that I'm more honest and my women are more beautiful."

"Part of the beauty of me is that I am very rich."

"I dealt with Qaddafi. I rented him a piece of land. He paid me more for one night than the land was worth for two years, and then I didn't let him use the land."

"Number one, I have great respect for women. I was the one that really broke the glass ceiling on behalf of women"

These quotes (and much of what he says and writes in tweets) boldly display:

1. An appalling lack of understanding of issues/technologies/events/history/the world...

2. An appalling lack of awareness of his own shortcomings and deficits.

3. An appalling (and child-like) lack of awareness of a world beyond himself.

He could do great damage to the world within four years if he stays energetic, active, engaged, provocative and disruptive.

But clearly he has a short attention span and he doesn't particularly like to read, work, study, or listen. So while he is watching cable news, golfing and dining at Mar a Lago, some contemporary Rasputins (Bannon for one) will be able to do great damage to the world.

We are about to find out just how solid and resilient and principled American Democracy really is.

Analyzing Trump Gibberish Session 33

April 3, 2017

When speaking to someone, perhaps answering a question, most of us occasionally go off on a tangent, we find the first clause of our thought and sentence has triggered a parallel thought. Many of us find at times that the thought, the idea we were expressing, requires a change of format, a change of sentence structure in the middle of the utterance in order that it make sense. At that point we pause, and then either find a link such as "about which" that will work, or we start over and restructure from the beginning. Sometimes we realize what we said was not clear, and then reformulate the thought with, "What I am trying to say is...". Sometimes the whole sentence is verbalized before we realize that it doesn't quite work as a logical thought.

But always, or almost always, we notice this ourselves, during the time we are talking or immediately after. That is, we listen to ourselves.

And this is one of the things perplexing about Donald J. Trump. **He either doesn't listen to himself or he doesn't care what comes out of his mouth.**

A recent New York Times article called it gibberish and indicative of some sort of derangement.

We are all capable of gibberish at times. What worries me is that Donald Trump does not seem to notice he is speaking gibberish. This may explain the ease with which he lies and contradicts himself.

I don't really understand this. His narcissism, yes. His short attention span, yes. His lazy grandiosity, yes. But what does it mean when the President of the United States does not listen to himself when he speaks? What does it mean when he does not listen to himself and notice the inconsistencies and contradictions in his speech, when he loses his way mid-sentence? Apart from being dangerous for the rest of us?

In a state of **mania** a rapid stream of consciousness occurs, a flight of tangential thinking, "pressured speech" as we call it, random thoughts

74

and exhortations, sometimes linked only by rhythm and rhyme. But President Trump is not manic.

I have spent many years listening to **delusions**. Clear, simple, "fixed" delusions (as we call them) contain an inner logic. Trump's speech patterns do not contain an inner logic. By inner logic I mean that if one accepts the hypothesis that the Martians are controlling me, then all else that I assert on this subject is plausible, if I can logically link it to the central idea.

Fractured, unsettled, probing, scanning, **disorganized delusional thinking** is different. It is a brain frantically looking for an organizing principle. This comes closer to Trump speak, but he does not appear in any other way to be psychotic.

Sprinkling random observations into the middle of an exchange and then forgetting you have done this can be a sign of **dementia**.

"The snow is on the ground."

"Mother, it's July."

"I know that."

"Then why did you mention snow?"

"I didn't say anything about snow."

This is probably not the problem afflicting Donald Trump, but time will tell. If it is some form of dementia it will get worse.

And then, just recently in the Oval Office while holding a conference with some members of Congress, he announced, in relation to the battle for Mosul, and specifically the involvement of American troops, "they are fighting like they've never fought before." He said this with a particular tone and prosody, and a smile of pleasure, of good news and high expectations.

It is an interesting phrase in that context, rather meaningless and perhaps somewhat insulting to the veterans of the Iraq war and many other wars. Except if you take the phrase and the contextual information together, the unspoken portion of this thought ends with, **"because I am an inspiration to them."**

It is similar to other favorite phrases of his, such as "like you've never seen before". "It will make your head spin."

It is empty salesmanship, a promise of nothing really, and a way of taking credit if something good happens, a way of congratulating himself in advance.

And it shows a paucity of complex thought beyond that of a 14 year old.

Linguists point out that the ability to compose and utter a sentence consisting of several clauses, with a premise supported by observations, leading to a logical conclusion, is a product of reading. Prior to written language all we required was something like, "Lion come, run." But Trump's performance with the teleprompter demonstrates that he can read, he just doesn't read much. This leads some pundits and scholars to point out that we are in a post-print age. That much of Mr. Trump's base do not read either.

Still, one would think Mr. Trump would notice when he is talking gibberish. And I would think it is the moral duty of all those who get to interview him, to point it out.

We live in a new age, when the spoken words (and tweets) of one man are instantly shared with the world, and because of his position of power, they have impact, they have weight. But while the world is listening to this man, he is not listening to himself.

The silver lining to this is, I think, that the Merkels, Mays, Trudeaus of this world have figured it out: that all his utterances, lies, contradictions, illogical constructions, and gibberish, can be translated as, simply, **"I am great and you are not."**

But this also means he can be easily manipulated by the Putins and Bannons of this same world.

Mini Quiz – Are you Prone to Populism? Session 34

April 7, 2017

The men (I don't think I can accurately say men and women) who came up with our Canadian Senate (the house of sober second thought) and the complex set of checks and balances of the American Republic knew we humans were, at least quite often, drunken, impulsive, short-sighted, and stupid. They knew we often react emotionally, that we throw logic to the wind, that we forget history. They knew that we, like mice, despite hearing the snap of a trap to our left or right, still go for the cheese. We still buy the snake oil. We still go along with the mob and chant whatever the mob is chanting.

Below is a small test to prove this point. Please answer quickly according to that first impulse, the one Populist leaders count on.

1. A lane jumper on the three lane highway pulls in front of you, slams on his brakes causing you to do the same and spill your medium regular Tim Horton's coffee in your lap.

He should be:

A. Taken out and shot

B. Bitch slapped

C. Have his driver's license revoked forever

D. Given a small admonishing toot of your horn.

2. A man is convicted of killing a child.

He should be:

A. Taken out and shot

B. Castrated, put in a rat infested cell, and then taken out and shot.

C. Allowed to appeal on a technicality.

D. Sentenced to life with no chance of parole for 10 years.

3. For the fourth time this summer your neighbour has dumped his tree trimmings on your side of the fence.

He should be:

A. Taken out and shot

B. The recipient of three of your bags of garbage.

77

C. Cursed at under your breath.

D. Forgiven because, after all, the rather dirty Mulberry tree is yours.

4. A young man has broken into your house, stolen your jewelry, smashed your crockery, and swilled your 20 year old Scotch. He should be:

A. Taken out and shot.

B. Sent back to Jamaica.

C. Offered a community recreation center.

D. Face due process like everyone else.

5. A salesman talks your aging mother into buying a very expensive furnace she does not need.

He should be:

A. Taken out and shot

B. Tied in a gerry chair and left in the corner of a dementia ward.

C. Arrested for fraud

D. Be reported to the Chamber of Commerce and receive a letter from your lawyer.

6. Illegal immigrants

Should be:

A. Taken out and shot

B. Rounded up and dumped in some other country.

C. Put in detention cells for 2 years and then dumped in some other country.

D. Offered a specific monitored pathway to achieve citizenship within a reasonable time frame.

7. Hillary is just a little too smug and prissy in her boxy white pant suit.

She should be:

A. Taken out and shot.

B. Locked up for life

C: Given I.T. and fashion advice

D. Elected anyway because she is actually competent

8. Those uppity Germans and Snooty French are having too big a say in how we live in England.

They should be:

A. Taken out and shot.

B. Delivered divorce papers

78

C. Asked to accommodate our peculiarities a little more in the E.U. parliament.

D. Asked to remind us why we organized the common market and E.U. in the first place.

I am Distressed to Hear the War Drums Session 35

April 17, 2017

I am distressed to hear the war drums. I am distressed listening to the talking heads, the panel of retired generals, pundits, and experts on CNN talk of war with North Korea. I am distressed by their matter-of-factness, by their strategic and political ponderings, all so devoid of horror.

How do we remain so inured to the real consequences of war?

My grandfather died in 1972. I had long thought he fought at Vimy, and on a visit there, to see the trenches and the monument, I wrote in the guest book, "I came to see where my grandfather fought." In the trenches and the bomb craters one can smell the fear, sense the horror, see the threat of opposing trenches a stone's throw away. At the monument, awe and pride intrude. My grandfather was here.

But it turns out he wasn't.

Thanks to the wonders of the digital age I now have 93 adobe pages of my grandfather's military record from the moment he enlisted until his discharge and the time of his death.

He enlisted in January of 1915 and joined the Canadian Expeditionary Force when it was still necessary for a married man to have his wife's permission. His wife and my grandmother was Irene Alice who he left behind in Victoria with three children. A fourth would arrive, at least by my calculations, after the war.

On the enlistment form, just above a final declaration, is a curious question: "Do you understand the nature and terms of your engagement?" He answered "yes" and then completed the form with a signature much like my father's and my own. He was 28 years old and five foot nine. He was assigned to the 30th battalion and sent overseas in the spring of 1915. From January 1915 until March 31, 1916 my grandmother received between 30 and 40 dollars per month.

He spent the summer training at Shorncliffe, on the Kentish coast of England, and then, in September, he was shipped to the front. The front being the trenches of France, and then Belgium and the second battle of Ypres.

Twice in France he was taken from the trenches to a field hospital suffering from influenza. He was promoted to Sergeant by late September 1915, and then to Sergeant Major. Upon discharge he was awarded the Distinguished Service Medal.

On June 3, 1916, at the Battle of Mont Sorrel, within the second battle of Ypres, my grandfather rose from the trench at the call to charge. A bullet pierced his right bicep and shrapnel hit him in the right side of his face. He was evacuated to the Graylingwell War Hospital with "wounds to his right arm and scalp".

In the documents I have the army is more detailed and thorough in its descriptions of the pay records than either combat or medical experiences, but I do have terse notes by doctors and digitized versions of the original x-rays.

My grandfather's right arm healed quickly. The x-rays show a piece of shrapnel behind the right eye lodged in bone. They did not attempt to remove this. He is transferred to a convalescent hospital with his arm healed and almost fully functional but suffering from poor sleep (nightmares of his time in the trenches), headaches and dizzy spells. The dizzy spells cause him to black out and fall frequently. Specialists cannot find a physical cause to explain these latter symptoms and they diagnose the etiology as, in part, "nervous".

By August of that year he is declared medically unfit to return to duty and then formally discharged from the army in January, 1917. The monthly pay to my grandmother ceases two months later.

So he did fight in the trenches; he was wounded, and he was furloughed to London as I knew, but he didn't fight at Vimy as I had come to believe. And it is 30 to 40 years later that I formed my first memories of my grandfather and he never spoke of the war and I had no idea of the questions I might ask.

But now my medical curiosity has kicked in. Initially his symptoms might have been concussive, or post concussive. Next he certainly suffered from what they called "nerves" and would soon refer to as "shell shock" and now PTSD. He did suffer the living hell of the cold muddy trenches in France and Belgium through the winter of 1916. He watched men dying suddenly. He watched men dying slowly. He watched men throw themselves into battle to relieve their growing terror.

But it is also possible that he continued to report dizzy spells and he continued to fall down at the convalescent hospital because he did not want to go back to those trenches.

Perhaps he had come to know that in war there is no glory to be had.

Parenting Kim Jong Un and Donald J Trump Session 36

April 19, 2017

As every parent knows for a threat to be effective the child must believe his father or mother will make good the threat if he does not comply. The child also knows that when the threat is outrageous ("you will be banned from all electronics for life.") it is also hollow. Still, some children do not listen to threats even when they are consistently followed by reasonable consequences. This is often true of ADHD children, and those for whom the compulsion is too great (OCD) or the aversion to change too strong (ASD).

By the time children are teens the plot thickens. Now they are watching themselves through the eyes of their peers, not just their parents. Now they are clinging to new visions of themselves as capable, independent sentient beings with newly formed logical thinking processes. They are more apt to defy the threat if to comply would undermine this developing sense of self.

And then we have adults. And now for a threat to work it must overcome all the above plus pride if this all occurs privately and secretly, and much more if the threat occurs publicly (shame and loss of face), and more so still if the threatened figure is a man or woman whose sense of self, if not his very existence, depends on the adulation of the crowd.

There are public figures in this world whose behaviour we would like to change. Perhaps there are some of these whose sanity, whose internal stability and strength is sufficient to bring about a good response to threat.

Kim Jong Un is not one of them.

Please do not threaten this man. Never publicly threaten him. He will not respond as you wish him to.

Actually, Donald Trump may just be the right President for the task of soothing North Korea. He could invite Kim to Mar a Lago for a Korean BBQ and treat him like royalty. Let him expound. Set up a private communication system. Help him be more of a hero to his people by feeding and housing them better. Then privately discuss reducing his nuclear arsenal for something in return.

Of course this would require Donald to keep his own ego in check. Vain hope.

Could it be time for Canada to step in here. Are you listening Justin? Making Kim look weak and foolish before his own people could get millions killed. We need a Mike Pearson way of intervening now.

And all of you, including Pence and others saying that your patience is at an end, pay heed to the words of a much smarter man than yourself:

"Talk, talk, talk is better than war, war, war." – Winston Churchill.

Please Stop Listening to Donald Trump Session 37

April 24, 2017

There was a point in my mother's dementia when she could engage in a ten minute conversation with an acquaintance or stranger without the person discovering that she, my mother, could not tell you her address, age, the date or day of the week. She was adept at the speechisms, the smiles, the nods, the all-purpose declarations of pleasantness, of good weather, of well being, of the "So nice to see you again", "lovely weather we're having" kind of remark.

In a perverse sort of way it reminds me of Donald. Though his fill-ins, rather than being pleasantries, are a rather random assortment of extreme declarations: bad, very bad, terrible, horrible, disastrous, disgraceful to wonderful, terrific, great, best, like you've never seen before.

Note that both "lovely weather we're having" and "like you've never seen before" work adequately no matter the reality.

Donald probably knows his addresses (they are easy to remember), the date, his handicap, the names of his children, but he clearly knows little else. His throwaway statements of "big league" and "disaster" stir his audience, but they also hide a chasm of knowledge and a lack of any detailed understanding.

We can be sure that when he rants about the dairy industry, Canada, and NAFTA, he knows nothing about these subjects. When he tells Fox News interviewer Maria Bartiromo about the "most beautiful piece of chocolate cake you've ever seen" and how he leaned across and told the President of China that he had just launched 59 missiles "at Iraq", it wasn't a slip of the tongue in a rapid conversation. Maria corrected him, simply saying, "You mean Syria?" He repeated her "Syria" without blinking, and went back to talking about dessert.

But he is POTUS and so the pundits, politicians, reporters, experts, panel members all try to find meaning, thought, policy, and direction in his utterances. Beside my own mother's dementia it conjures images of courtiers, earls, and nobles trying to find wisdom in an idiot king's sighs and passing of gas.

I think Trudeau and Merkel understand this. Let's hope Kim, Xi, and Vladimir do as well.

You're Wonderful, Mr. Trump, But War is a Really Bad Thing
Session 38

May 1, 2017

I apologize for being so obsessed with Donald Trump but with the doomsday clock being closer to midnight than ever before, with a rekindling of cold war tensions, with Noam Chomsky worried, the arid lands expanding, the oceans rising, this one incompetent man is in a position to do extraordinary harm to our planet.

However, an aspect of his personality seems to be emerging that I had not guessed would be there. Despite his bluster, his threats, his word salad provocations, when someone meets with him face to face he quickly backs down, changes his "mind".

General Mattis convinced him that maybe torture was not a good thing. Someone else explained to him that health care systems are complicated. Someone else explained NATO to him and that perhaps it is not so obsolete after all. Trump meets with the President of China and China is no longer a currency manipulator. And now phone calls from Justin Trudeau and Enrique Pena Nieto have caused him to pass on withdrawing from NAFTA.

Which means several things:
1. That bluster of confidence and narcissism is a thin veneer.
2. A very insecure man lies beneath.
3. Above all he wants to be liked, loved, respected.
4. Face to face he quickly backs down.

So this means to keep our world safe and secure, the adults in the room need merely take him aside and talk to him. And others not in the room should finagle an invitation to Mar a Lago.

Unfortunately it also means that when his bluster and off-the-cuff proposals align with the self-interest of the only adults in the room they are unlikely to have that talk with him.

So America is stuck with a massive increase in military spending, fewer regulations, much less environmental protection, more tax breaks and benefits for billionaires, some fracking here and there, a little more oil and coal, a little less wild life, a few more guns – and those boys in uniform we call The Military, well, they may get to play with a few of their favorite toys. (Such as the MOAB and Tomahawks)

Then I watched "At Issue" on CBC. And although the panel on CBC is so much more gracious, thoughtful, and polite than any counterpart on CNN, they still seek meaning and planning in the words of Donald Trump. Like he actually thought these things out. Like he actually plans his flip-flops. As if he might actually be two moves ahead on the chessboard. NO. Just listen carefully to any extended interview. He knows almost nothing. He has no plan. He has no convictions. He cannot sustain a thought of any complexity.

He's like a kid who once took an angry swipe at his pile of blocks, causing them to break the jar on the counter, which then poured chocolate jellybeans upon him. He spends his life trying to repeat this. I think the shrinks call it repetition-compulsion.

But here is the silver lining and my advice to all sane, sensible, reasonable, liberal, thoughtful leaders in this world. Don't react to his tweets, his bluster. Don't engage through media. Meet him face to face. Show him respect. Then tell him, respectfully, what he should do, and why. And smile all the while.

Justin, I think you are just the right man for this assignment.

The Real Reason James Comey Was Fired Session 39

May 10, 2017

CNN interviewees offered these three competing explanations last night:

1.   That he has lost the confidence of the public and law enforcement? An unlikely cause for a summary dismissal.

2.   That he mishandled the Clinton email problem one year ago? No. C'mon now. Trump would not fire Comey for that reason. Never.

3.   That the investigation he leads is closing in on the Trump-Russia connection? Well, Doh.

But there is a fourth, slightly less portentous possibility.

James Comey, in his recent testimony to Congress, said:

"It makes me mildly nauseous to think we might have had some impact on the election."

Donald Trump won that election. So to paraphrase, Comey testified, before the world, that, **"He feels sick to his stomach when he thinks he may have helped Trump get elected."**

Donald just might have taken that personally. He tends to do that.

With Trump – The Devil is in the Details Session 40

May 12, 2017

As the political theater continues south of our border, lurching toward a constitutional crisis, everybody is weighing in, asking every conceivable question, offering every conceivable opinion.

For part of this though, at least when it comes to Donald Trump, we need but listen closely.

Did he ask Comey if he, Donald J. Trump, was under investigation?

Did Comey answer?

Is any of this normal, ethical, proper? Might it even be obstruction of justice?

Is it true?

Listen and read carefully.

The truth, I think, lies in his use of the modifier 'three'. As in **"three times"** Comey told him he was not under investigation.

This is not something he should have asked the Chief investigator of himself and his cronies, and the Chief investigator should not have answered. But did this actually happen even once?

The "three times" wording indicates the whole thing is a simple lie. A childish lie. An unnecessary embellishment. The kind of embellishment and exaggeration a child uses to sell his lie.

It is the kind of embellishment and gross exaggeration Trump always uses to sell his lies. "You know it, I know it, everybody knows it."

As I have said before, during the impeachment process please take away the nuclear codes.

And this morning, it was suggested that Trump may be intimidating a witness http://www.politicususa.com/2017/05/12/donald-trump-intimidate-witness-threat-james-comey.html

What To Do When King Donald Goes Mad Session 41

May 22, 2017

In November of 2016 I wrote the piece that follows. <u>Predictions for the Trump Presidency.</u> As Donald himself might say, "Who knew impeachment was so complicated?" So, I got that wrong. It will be a long and messy process. If only they had a parliamentary system and could simply call for a vote of non-confidence.

And I did not guess the extent to which Trump would incriminate himself with both his careless tweets and his loose boastful talk in both the Russia affair and the obstruction of investigation into the Russia affair.

Other than that though, my predictions are depressingly accurate. And I still think the danger for the U. S. of A. and the rest of the world is that Donald Trump, unlike Nixon, will not go gentle into that good night. The sane and rational leaders of America need a plan. As the bad news mounts; when Trump's counter attacks and deflections begin to fail; when he is cornered, he will lash out. They must make sure he cannot bring the temple down.

<u>Predictions for the Trump Presidency</u>
By Dr David Laing Dawson (Nov. 24, 2016)
The good news:
Donald Trump has neither the knowledge nor patience to figure out how to repeal parts of Obamacare, renegotiate NAFTA, build a great wall, prosecute Hillary, create the mechanisms to actually find and deport 3 million immigrants, or even change the tax system.

He won't interfere much with climate change accords, because he doesn't really care one way or the other and this is also a very complicated endeavor. He will continue to contradict himself from day to day, responding to his immediate impulses and his (I must admit) well honed intuitions about his public.

91

He can interfere with the TPP because all he has to say is, "Not gonna do it." China can take the lead and a trade deal will be struck with all countries on the Pacific excluding the USA. I have no idea what that means for the USA or Canada.

Anything that requires a great deal of work, attention to detail, building a consensus, formulating a complex plan, he will not do.

The bad news:

Within a few weeks of his presidency Donald Trump will manage to mix his business dealings, his self-aggrandizement, and his petty peeves with his presidency, with his representation of the people of the United States, to such a degree that the democrats and a few republicans will start an impeachment process. In the ensuing hearings his business dealings around the world and at home will be exposed. He will respond with anger and outrageous accusations. This will convince others to support the impeachment.

As it becomes clear that Donald J. Trump will be successfully impeached he will become a raging bull. He will not simply announce, "I am not a crook." and board the helicopter in disgrace. He will rage. He will suffer an extreme blow to his narcissism. He will rage and lash out.

This will fuel the racist fires at home and cause great anxiety abroad. He could well bring the temple down.

Sane American leaders need to be thinking about a contingency plan.

Perhaps the fully sane leaders of the rest of the world could form a club and plan a contingency of their own. What to do when King Donald goes mad.

Standing By Trump – Or Not Session 42

May 24, 2017

As social scientists point out, it is a prime directive for homo sapiens to maintain standing in their community (power, pecking order, value); it is not a prime directive to listen to reason and apply educated perceptual and deductive processes to arrive at a truth. Hence the amazing displays of twisting, selecting, avoiding, diverting, and denial coming from Republican law makers when asked to comment on a particularly stupid, childish or even incriminating comment by Donald Trump.

In the Hans Christian Andersen story it is only a child who is free to blurt out, "But the emperor has no clothes." The lords, the noblemen, the ladies, the merchants – they all have much to lose. As does the emperor himself.

This emperor, The Donald, likewise has much to lose should he ever admit either ignorance or failure. His whole narcissistic edifice would crumble. He would find himself staring at a reality he has never allowed himself to see before.

And perhaps some of those Republicans do not have law degrees or other marketable skills, and rely on their Government salaries to support five children, an invalid wife, two aging parents, and a large mortgage. These I forgive. They should keep their heads down and avoid microphones. But there are others I am sure who have many options. They would lose but the ephemeral status of a title and invitations to the old boys club.

Yet none speak up.

It is disappointing to learn that in an old democracy an incompetent man can be elected President on the basis of misdirected anger, show business glitz, and ridiculous promises, all flavored with misogyny and racism.

But it is more disappointing to see that not one nobleman, not one lawmaker, is able to overcome the prime directive from our days in the jungle – not one has the courage to put his standing in his community at risk and announce, as the child would, "The emperor has no clothes. The emperor is lying. The emperor is incompetent. I can no longer support the emperor. I resign."

Short Unofficial Profiles of the People Around Trump
Session 43

June 7, 2017

Sessions: Obsequious little man who hides his hatred beneath an endearing smile and a soft southern drawl. Iago comes to mind. But Donald is not Othello. Think Richard III instead.

Kushner: Unreadable age, temperament and intentions. A Mona Lisa smile. No apparent anxiety, worry, puzzlement, or humour. That degree of control and confidence in what should be overwhelming complex human situations can only be explained by psychopathy. If this were a kingdom and he were next in line for the crown he would be plotting the death of the King already. Perhaps he is.

Bannon: I know this man, but not in a position of power. Intellectually brilliant, alone in his squalid rooming house, paying no attention to hygiene or diet as he pores over history and its many conspiracies, iterations and cycles to arrive at his own nihilistic philosophy in which mankind destroys itself and he can then look upon the rubble knowing that he is close to being a God.

Pence: A child-like belief in God and destiny, so much so that he can forgive the most egregious sins and comfort himself that it must all be part of God's plan, even if it elevates him to a position for which he is not remotely qualified, and even if it casts him among sinners.

Ivanka: Though perhaps a little smarter than her father and perhaps slightly more empathetic, she has otherwise inherited or absorbed his tone-deaf sense of entitlement. I can hear her say, when told the peasants have no bread, "Let them eat cake." Or at least, "Tell them to architect their own destiny as I have."

Tillerman: A blunt and successful force in the business world, he became depressed when confronted by the daunting task of being Secretary of State for a naked emperor. He, alone among the group,

95

realizes he has much to learn about government and nations. He will soon have a crisis of conscience. He knows he is on stage in "The Scottish Play".

Spicer: Sean is a lost soul approaching the gates of hell. He knows it is too late. Ignominy awaits if he rejects Satan now. Ignominy awaits if he continues on this path. He will one day die the Death of Ivan Illych, tormented by his cowardice and his failure of conscience.

Conway: Kellyanne is Madam Bovary, trading on looks and charm, attaching to the man in the room who is most likely to bring her fame and fortune, luxury and TV time. She will happily say whatever pleases this man, easily convincing herself that truth is an overrated commodity. As her looks fade she will have to trade more on her willingness to flatter and lie. And she knows that when her Lord falls under the knives of impeachment she will be a welcome guest on all the talk shows.

Paul Ryan: A career politician since his days as student council president. The gift of a hollow smile and a brain always calculating the vectors of power. Honesty, ethics, morality, reality all fall beneath the sword of political expedience. He is something of an Ayn Rand libertarian, which really means, "Let no agency have power, unless it is I." and "I'm all right Jack; so bugger the rest of you."

Kim Jong-Un Goes to the White House Session 44

June 14, 2017

In our histories there were times the mad arrogant king could demand that his subjects, especially the Lords and Ladies of his court, prostrate themselves in obedience and offer unlimited praise of his highness. They would do this because to refuse brought about death for themselves and a life of penury or slavery for their families.

To my knowledge Donald Trump does not have such powers (yet). But still his cabinet engaged in such a ritual display before the world. As if from a script they each in turn offered the same words of honour and subservience, rounding off with a fantastical account of the state of the nation, the world, and their particular spheres of influence, and indebtedness to his majesty.

I could only listen to a few of these and perhaps, maybe, someone in the circle diverged from the script later. The last to speak I listened to described such a delusional world view I could watch no more.

This is not something we should be watching in a democracy. Perhaps North Korea, or Saudi Arabia, not America. The penalty for not complying, of thinking for themselves, of being principled and honest is not death. At least not yet. Where is their pride? Where is their courage?

More importantly, if they do not find this courage soon, the day may come when the penalty for disobedience will be death and a life of penury for their children

The Doctor gives us one hundred years Session 45

June 21, 2017

What an interesting time to be alive. I had grandparents who drove some of the first mass produced automobiles; parents who listened to the radio, took penicillin, and flew in planes; I grew up among a generation of boys who dismantled cars and rebuilt them to drive when we got our licenses at 16; we watched television going from black and white to colour, and analogue to digital, from large boxes to thin screens; we bought 64K computers; watched the first messages pass through the internet and modems; watched portable phones, libraries, laptop computers, arcades, cameras, pagers, slide rules, and calculators merge into this ubiquitous instrument we call a smart phone; we learned to say double helix, and then genome; we saw small amounts of data stored on microfiche evolve into terrabytes of data stored in something smaller than a thumbnail; my son and daughter work in the high tech industries; my grandson is studying artificial intelligence at University; and Stephen Hawking tells us we need to colonize another planet or two within 100 years or risk extinction.

If he is right, then the generations alive today are humans who have links to the early days of mass production in the industrial revolution, to the beginnings and early evolution of modern science, medicine, and agricultural practices, right though the digital age, space travel, and on to the destruction of the planet.

Our dramatic success over the past few generations (give or take some stupid wars, genocides and catastrophes) is leading directly to the demise of our species, all within a dozen generations. That is impressive if sad.

Hawking includes possible "acts of God" in his list of destructive forces (direct hit by a large meteor) but most scenarios include one form of suicide or another (pandemic spread around the globe, nuclear holocaust, the consequences of over population, and global warming).

Biologically our evolution has spanned millions of years. Until the industrial revolution our social evolution had been almost as slow and incremental. Capitalism, democracy, science, medicine, and technology have jet propelled (literally and figuratively) this social evolution the past 150 years.

Before then we were creatures surviving within a complex ecology, our population very slowly increasing, subject to the whims of weather, drought, wars, and pestilence. We had minimal effect on our planet. We could build a boat, a city, a canal, and a damn, but the oceans and forests continued, the rivers, deserts, and most of our earth's life forms persisted. To survive through those centuries we needed to expand, explore, conquer, and exploit.

Not now.

Now quite suddenly we are the shepherds of our own destiny as a species, a life form. To survive we must all cooperate. We must give up notions of magic and Gods and competing feifdoms. We must stop population growth through all humane means of birth control. We must husband our planet's resources rather than exploit them. We must have in place an international program ready to act instantly when the next pestilence arises. We must stop talking about economic growth and replace this with equitable economic distribution. We must stop destroying our oceans and forests. And of course we must either reduce our CO_2 emissions or figure out how to capture them.

A tall order. Especially when some leaders of our fully industrialized nations want to pull us back to an age of competing xenophobic fiefdoms. A hundred years is but a blink of a galaxy's eye.

Dump Trump Session 46

June 30, 2017

If a doctor, teacher, manager, administrator of 70 years of age emailed, announced, or tweeted what Donald Trump just tweeted I would immediately suspect alcohol or frontal lobe dementia. Besides being relieved of his office, or license, his family would take him to a family doctor who might then refer him to either an addiction service or a psychiatrist/neurologist. It would be a striking failure of judgment only plausibly explained by frontal lobe impairment.

With Donald Trump though, this kind of behaviour is not new or unusual. But even a narcissistic misogynistic sociopath might recognize that in the context of being POTUS such a tweet would bring only shame upon his head and reduce, not enhance, his status.

So we have to conclude that either Donald Trump is the same Donald Trump he has always been plus he now has some early dementia, or, his personality disorder is so severe, his ego so fragile, that he cannot stop himself from engaging in a playground (age 14 maybe) retaliation, even when it would be so obviously damaging to him, his family, and his country.

Either diagnosis bodes poorly for the safety of our planet. Please, Republicans, understand this man will take you down with him. It is time to act.

Although, while Trump may be a threat to all things good and sane, from what I see and read, the Republican party in its current form may be an equal or bigger threat to democracy.

Racism Session 47

July 3, 2017

At least three times per week every week, between editorials in my local paper and the CBC I am made to feel guilty about any vestiges of prejudice I might have, or even my ancestors might have had, toward people of a different race. I often get to the point where I mutter, "Enough already".

A fan of Star Trek has a vanity license plate with a form of "Assimilate" on it, the demand of The Borg. Someone objects for it is reminiscent of an attitude some of my ancestors had toward First Nations People. But we all know it is more complicated than that. To begin with The Borg are (or is) villain(s) in that Sci Fi series. And, despite the sense of loss felt by several generations, we all assimilate eventually, while retaining some ceremonial cultural practices and artifacts.

But perhaps we need to be scolded three times per week. For deep within the current political theater in the USA lurks the unmistakable venom of racism. Even the rush to a new health care bill is quite obviously being driven more by a wish to remove "The Stain" of having had a black president than any fervently held ideological position or humanitarian hope. It is there in the language used. It is there in the faces of the proponents of "Repeal and Replace".

It is there in the stroke of Trump's pen and the triumphant faces behind him when he signs off on orders to stop anything Obama started, no matter how innocuous, or, for that matter, no matter how obviously good it was. It is there in the tendency to excoriate anything achieved during the eight years Barack Obama was president. It is there in the ignoring of Sally Yates' wise counsel. It is there in the attitude toward Sanctuary cities and Urban police. It is there in the sea of old white male faces standing behind Trump in the Oval Office. It is there in the soft and reluctant criticism of white supremacist groups. It is there in the activities of ICE.

When Trump claims the world "**was** laughing at us" this is code for "the world was laughing at us because we elected a black president."

So, despite my first paragraph, despite my occasional irritation with excess political correctness, keep scolding us please, keep reminding us. It looks like we all need this if we are not to willfully or accidentally step on that slippery slope back to tribalism and contempt for those unlike ourselves.

102

"Is Donald Trump Human?" Session 48

July 7, 2017

Men in Black, from 1997, with Will Smith and Tommy Lee Jones, is full of good moments. The particular moment that came to mind, for reasons that will become apparent, follows the recruitment of Will Smith to the very small and select team. Tommy Lee is showing Will Smith the ropes. He suggests they "check the hot sheets". They stop by a News Stand to pick up a couple of tabloids, each with a lurid headline.

"These are the hot sheets?" asks Will.

"Best reporting on the planet," says Tommy. "Go ahead, read the New York Times if you want. They get lucky sometimes."

Smith spells out the gag: "I believe you are looking for tips in the supermarket tabloids."

Their headlines include: "Pope a Father", "Top Doctors baffled, Baby Pregnant", "Man Eats Own House" and "Alien Stole My Husband's Skin."

The scene is played straight.

It is a very funny moment, I thought.

And I have always assumed that anyone reading these yellow sheets is engaging in a guilty pleasure. They are titillating themselves with implausible stories. Today those titles would be called 'click bait'.

The publishers of these magazines, when they deal with celebrities, are marketing to our schadenfreude. Ah, how we enjoy reading that the lives of the rich and privileged may be as fraught with conflict and unhappiness, sin and regret, as our own.

But we know that when the story is not an outright lie, a gross exaggeration or invasion of privacy, it is still merely trivial. At least I thought we all understood that.

Hence the entire audience in the theater watching *Men in Black* got the joke.

But not, apparently, Donald Trump.

It is very distressing to learn that he and the publisher of The National Enquirer are good friends who influence one another. And that this publisher is thinking of buying Time Magazine.

There is a strange slippage afoot. I'm not sure whether we should be boning up on George Orwell or Lewis Carroll.

And I notice another thing entirely by accident. These Men in Black, American enforcement officers for true aliens, extraterrestrial aliens, of all shapes and sizes, some cute, some grotesque, some "legal" and some "illegal", treat these aliens with much more decency and respect than Donald Trump and ICE treat human "aliens."

"I Think Anthony Will Do Amazing" Session 49

August 7, 2017

In his brief sojourn in public life Anthony Scaramucci managed to provide hours of material for the late night shows and many columns of commentary by serious pundits.

It is all so troubling and disturbing. A man so obviously unqualified to be a Communications Director quickly drops the tenor of the office to the level of teen boy locker room talk in an under founded school system.

He has come and gone.

But within all the inaccuracies, lies, egoism, and stupidity of Donald Trump's statements in an interview with the Wall Street Journal on July 25, this particular use of language stood out for me:

"I think Anthony will do amazing."

There is a time in one's development of intellectual and linguistic abilities when nouns and adverbs and adjectives get all mixed up, when the brain cannot yet formulate explanatory secondary clauses, and when the brain does not yet notice the misuse of words, catch this, and then explain further.

That age is about 13, 14, 15. (and younger than this of course)

13, 14, 15 is the age at which I hear kids use the phrase, "will do amazing."

By 17, if they say "will do amazing" they catch themselves and explain further in a second clause, such as, "I mean, like, I think he will get really high marks."

By university level they realize that the quality of being amazed belongs to the observer, not the doer, and the whole thing is phrased differently.

And all through the transcripts of recent interviews and off-the-teleprompter speeches it is clear Donald Trump does not catch his own absurdities, his own unfinished thoughts, his own deviations from logic, and his own outrageous boasting.

105

I hear the same from 14-year-olds in my clinical practice. By 17 or so, most have the ability to hear what they have just said, to notice when it veers from truth or logic.

My American friends, your president is a very narcissistic entitled 14 year old.

Though, I must admit, as damaging as he is to the reputation of America in the rest of the world, he may be less dangerous than many Republican alternatives.

Might I suggest a strategy to keep us all safe: Every other leader in this fragile world of ours should send Donald Trump an effusive Valentine card four times a year, at least.

Fire and Fury Session 50

August 7, 2017

Some years ago the person who oversaw both the men's and women's shelters in this city expressed his surprise that far more actual physical fights broke out in the women's shelter than in the men's.

But it did make perfect sense after we discussed it.

Some irritation would occur, expected when living on top of one another, and a man would verbally insult another man. Then a pattern of behaviour would unfold that was learned on the playgrounds of every public school, playing field and back alley, one that probably has genetic roots we can observe with our cousins, the apes and chimpanzees.

"Yeah, and who's gonna make me?"

"You and who's army?"

Chin thrust forward, the baring of teeth, the snarl, the threatened encroachment on the other's space, insulting the other's sexuality, his courage, his birth, his mother, name calling, dire threats for the future, the unfurling of plumage.

Other men (boys) would intervene pulling the two apart as they hurled their last insults at one another. Their assuaging words were always of the order of, "He ain't worth it."

This last part is important, for it is face saving for both antagonists. And an actual fight is averted. Life goes on.

In the women's shelter, one would insult the other, and the recipient of the insult would hurl herself at the antagonist. They had not experienced the same playground socialization.

I am thinking about this because of Kim Jong Un and Donald Trump and the way war begins, and even those words of Tillerson and others, "It's the only language Kim Jong Un understands."

No. No. No.

Tillerson, your job is to put your arm around Donald Trump, pull him aside and say, "He ain't worth it."

Maybe no one can do that with Kim.

It doesn't matter. All that matters is that one of the protagonists, these blustering would-be alpha males, especially the stronger of the two, gets pulled back.

"Donald, he ain't worth it."

Now if American leadership really was smart and confident, it could offer Kim some face saving device. "But we will look weak," American leadership will scream. This despite the fact they have the capacity to destroy the world and we all know it.

Tillerson, you appear mostly sane to me, and a man who understands a few things. It is your job to pull Trump aside and tell him, "He ain't worth it. You could take him easy, but it ain't worth it."

And would it kill you to promise Kim that you will stop flying B 52's over North Korea and stop practicing war in South Korea if he stops testing A bombs?

On Democracy Session 51

August 7, 2017

In my childhood I took my birth certificate with me to sign up for a summer soccer league. Of course I lost it. There is a good chance I did not tell this to my parents. But three nights later we all responded to a knock on the door. Standing on the porch was a stocky man who proved to have a thick middle European accent and my birth certificate, a little grass stained.

I remember all this because he gave me a stern lecture about my birthright as a citizen in this democracy while I blushed under my father's gaze. Although, in my defense it was either my father or my mother who allowed me to take this precious piece of paper on my bike ride to the soccer field in the first place.

Among many others I have been writing about the threat to democracy Donald Trump and his colleagues pose as they systematically undermine the Fourth Estate, the judiciary, instill unease in the citizens, point their fingers at immigrants, and undermine the people's confidence in the electoral process.

But I did not think it would be so easy. Surely the very idea of free, regular, unfettered elections is sacrosanct in this American Democracy of which they are so proud.

Apparently not. A new poll finds that over 50 percent of Republicans would be quite happy to have the 2020 elections postponed if either Trump or the Republican Party suggested or requested this.

Wow. Should not their instinctive response be, "No way!"

So the groundwork has been laid. And apparently few Americans received the awakening I received in my childhood, a stern lecture from a man who escaped a tyranny, and who knew shortsightedness, indifference, and stupidity can lose a democracy but only bloodshed can regain it.

Trump's Great Service to Americans – But Time To Go Session 52

August 17, 2017

The unraveling of Donald Trump is nigh. And if it happens soon, and if the reaction he has provoked has staying power, then, surprisingly, Donald Trump will have performed a great service for America. Perhaps the reaction to Donald will bring about a better America.

Donald has brought to light the simmering racism, the unholy divide, and the hypocrisy that is America. It has always been there of course, addressed politely from time to time, but recently not so overtly, so publicly that it could not be ignored by others.

To be fair though, the credit probably goes equally to Barack Obama, for it may be this unusual sequence of a first black president, and a very good one, followed by a Donald Trump that so ignited the fires of white supremacists and then lifted the fog of denial from the eyes of liberals.

All of them, the KKK, the Nazis and neo-nazis, the white supremacists, they all quietly nursed their wounds and hatred during Obama's eight years. Now Donald has set them free.

On Tuesday, August 15, off the teleprompter, peppered with questions, Donald Trump revealed Donald. He was of course full of himself, referring back to his successes, even to his riches, boasting of his holdings, taking credit for an improved economy, defending his first statement after the events in Charlottesville, even taking it from his pocket and reading it again, even shamelessly claiming he received praise from the mother of the woman killed.

He became combative with the press, calling them fake news, stating he is more attentive and truthful than they are.

But most of all this exchange revealed his brittle narcissism and the extent to which he cannot tolerate any criticism, any possibility that he may not be the smartest, the best, the most successful person in the room, that he may have been imperfect this one time. And it revealed how his ego overshadows any concept of country, democracy, history. Asked if he would visit Charlottesville he told us he owns a house and a golf course there, the biggest, thus demonstrating his confusion between being president of a democracy and the emperor of all he surveys.

And it gave us a hint of how mad (this word meant to be read both ways) he will become when he is finally cornered and dethroned.

Do it soon. Do it carefully. Do it with a safety net in place.

Neo-nazis, Thugs, and Little Boys Session 53

August 28, 2017

In our history psychiatry overplayed its hand. As the theories of Freud, Jung, Adler and others caught on, some psychiatrists and psychologists thought we might have something to offer society as a whole. Perhaps psychological intervention could reduce violence generally, and even prevent war and promote peace.

This was overreach. And we are all aware now, I think, that the tools of psychiatry/psychology are more apt to be misused by the state (The Soviet Union), the CIA, Casinos, and by marketing, or building a better soldier, creating brand loyalty, selling junk food to kids, keeping a scholar or athlete focused.

For the most part the profession of psychiatry retreated to being a medical specialty engaged in the treatment of mental illness.

I was thinking of this while watching neo-nazi Christopher Cantwell on his Youtube video. He was an organizer and marcher in Charlottesville, and then a social media hit when he alternately ranted and sobbed on a self-produced video, after hearing there might be a warrant for his arrest.

Why any young and not-so-young American (or German or Canadian for that matter) might proclaim himself a Nazi today is a puzzle. As has been pointed out, they did not grow up watching their fathers lynch Negros or blame Jews for a recession. Where on earth does this come from?

But watching the performance of Christopher Cantwell it occurred to me that I had seen this many times before.

Troubled boys between age 14 and 17. Some ADHD, some labile emotions, and some developmental/cognitive immaturity. Within a half hour they might talk prison talk full of expletive laden revenge, need for respect, blame, threaten, and then cry, weep, apologize to me and their mothers. There is a frightened little boy inside that would-be thug.

They are trapped developmentally, still children dependent on adults, angry their needs are not immediately satisfied, experimenting with male roles of toughness, power, strength, (often borrowed from gang, drug, and prison cultures), ultimately terrified of adulthood and its demands for skills and responsibility.

Most get through this. Good parenting, time for the brain to develop and mature, some boundaries and structures that promote skill building and confidence, more self-reliance, less blaming of others. Sometimes pills for either ADHD or anxiety or both are required.

That is where Chris Cantwell is. I don't know how much he truly believes what he says, but he is still, developmentally, 14 to 17, at once angry, blaming, playing a macho role, labile and fearful.

So yes, good parenting, **some accessible mental health services**, the right school system, opportunities to develop skills and confidence, could reduce the number of young men who become neo-nazis, or terrorists for that matter.

The Women on the Right
Session 54

September 1, 2017

I am not puzzled by the heavy-set blowhard males who espouse the views of Briebart, Fox News, and the Alt right. I know them. I remember them. They were always loud, obnoxious, dripping with hostility, overcompensating for something: Didn't make the cut for the football team, passed over for Prom king, snubbed by the prettiest girl in the school, not dumb but certainly not first in the class, never cast in the lead of the school play.

But I have been puzzled by the females espousing the same views. The Ann Coulters of our television. But then I think, maybe I'm being sexist. Maybe I expect women to all be kind, empathetic, generous, inclusive, self-effacing. There is no reason a woman cannot be as selfish and short sighted and loud as a man. After all, their bible was written by a woman, one Ayn Rand.

Okay, adjust your thinking David. A woman has just as much right as a man to be a Roger Ailes, a Sean Hannity, a Glenn Beck, a Bill O'Reilly. Women can be loud, obnoxious, and right wing too.

But my puzzlement has returned, for yet another Fox News commentator has been suspended for "lewd photos sent to female colleagues."

My puzzlement is not about these men behaving socially and sexually as if their development was arrested at age 14. That goes with the territory. That is where they are.

It is all one and the same. Their sense of white male privilege extends to being lord of the jungle, having ownership of all they survey, and that includes the women folk. And their notion of courtship has always been to display plumage and induce fear.

But why don't the women recognize this? They are not and will never be equal partners in this right wing endeavor. Hand maids, concubines, and incubators, yes. But not equals.

So I remain puzzled by the women. Unless, of course, they have a plan to get rid of all the blowhard males and take over themselves.

Trump's Successful Assault on American Democracy
Session 55

October 2, 2017

At the very beginning of the Trump presidency I wrote a (I had hoped, satirical) set of instructions for undermining democracy. Nine months later some news items have prodded me to reread my instructions. Those news items were: 1. Justice department asking Facebook for information on people who "liked" an anti-administration protest page. 2. ICE agents arrest over 450 illegal immigrants in sanctuary cities. 3. Trump stokes racial division through the NFL. 4. Tax proposal to dramatically shift more wealth to the top 1%, including Trump himself. 5. A bill before the senate to loosen gun restrictions. (I didn't think they could be looser until reading the specifics, which include ending restrictions on selling silencers, concealed carry, and armor piercing ammunition).

It is time to revisit my instruction manual and see how Donald and America are progressing.

1. Make frequent reference to the utter failure of all previous administrations. Take credit for anything good that happened during the most recent administration. Done

2. Promote a cult of personality. Suggest the new leader has God-like powers, such as controlling the rain, and solving complex and intractable problems with forceful statements. Done

3. Paint a bleak picture of the current state of affairs and grossly exaggerate the risk, the dangers posed by outsiders and nonbelievers. Done

4. Promote law and order and military power as the only forces that can keep us safe. Done

5. Incrementally reduce voting rights by insisting on regulations that

favor your supporters and disenfranchise others. Do this by claiming you are controlling corruption and fraud. Done

6. Choose an enemy or two, give them names, and promise to eradicate them. Use emotionally inspiring words such as evil, kill, wipe them out, get rid of them once and for all. Done

7. Exaggerate the size of your support and the crowds attending your rallies. Refer to this as a movement. Done

8. Lie frequently and often. Use big, bold lies. This is a form of desensitization. More and more will believe your lies. The remaining citizens will stop caring. Done

9. Undermine the Fourth Estate. Seed distrust of news and information. Call all reporters and truth tellers liars. It will be difficult to fully control the media (this is not Russia) but consider using licensing bodies, libel laws and the courts to tie their hands. Done

10. Promote the idea that the people of your nation, your followers, are superior human beings, exceptional, and deserve to live better than others. American Exceptionalism. Or is that "Uber Alles"? Done

11. You will need the armed forces and intelligence agencies so flatter them frequently, while you replace their leaders with your own men. Done

12. You will need cabinet members and spokespeople who will unabashedly promote you and your statements and policies no matter how unpalatable or ludicrous they become. Some will be willing to do this for money, others for power and glory of their own, and others because of their own anger and resentment from earlier grievances. Unfortunately such people abound. But remember, it is not loyalty that binds them to you, but self-interest. Reward them generously; always be prepared to kill them. Done

13. Quickly disparage and render impotent any leader who opposes you. Memorable name-calling and disinformation will suffice. Done

14. Create a language of code words for anything that remains unacceptable for most citizens. For example: "alternative facts" for lies, "violence in the inner cities" for racial profiling. Done

15. Use hyperbole at all times. A person or event is either "great", "fantastic", "amazing", or "a disaster", "evil", "total failure". This fosters a dichotomous view of the world and will help dehumanize victims when the time comes to purge. Done

16. Find some allies in other countries by directly or tacitly supporting their extreme views. Examples might include Putin, Marine Penn and Netanyahu. Be unpredictable for the others. Keep them on edge. Done

17. In the meantime cater to the dominant political force in the democratic body by quickly implementing all their pet projects (e.g anti-abortion legislation), and by canceling all social and medical initiatives started by that upstart negro president . Done

18. Build monuments to yourself. Oops. I forgot. You already have. Good. Build more. Start with the Trump Great Southern Wall. Done

19. Throughout this process continue to emphasize that you are working for the people. Use the words "people", "working people" and "democracy" frequently. As you usurp power explain that you are protecting democracy. Done

20. Have patience. Others may deliver you the crisis and fear that will allow an incremental or bold increase in power. When you assume new powers present yourself as reluctant to do so. Done

21. Use as much pomp and circumstance as possible. People love ceremonies. Emphasize the sacred trust your office embodies. Done

22. Visit a religious leader (televised of course). Ensure him and the American Public that you understand the enormity of your office and the need for God's guidance. Try not to sneer or chuckle doing this. It is not wise to compare yourself to God, but you can hint that He favors you in some way. Done

23. Don't worry about the physical quirks the cartoonists seize upon, the little black mustache for example, or the blonde comb over. Ultimately these will confer upon you icon status. Done

24. There will be protests and marches against you. Be gracious in your response to those that remain peaceful. Come down very hard on those that become violent. Emphasize these, and use them to accrue more power. But, be assured that any large gathering of people can become violent with a little help from your friends. Done

25. Toady up to the leaders of organized religion, the church. With few exceptions these religious leaders will see you as a means of helping them achieve their long-term goals. They will not stand against you for fear of losing their own power. Done

26. Allow others to live vicariously through you. This is a fine balance.

118

While allowing the people to view your sumptuous life style use colloquial language, talk as they do. Remind them you work tirelessly for them. Pretend that one day they can all live as you do. Done

27. Women are tricky. Have one or two around you but not many. They tend to have empathy for others, children, small animals. They tend to prefer compromise and cooperation. Reference your own dear mother frequently, and say how much you respect women. But subtly denigrate them by your own actions, and limit their voices and rights through reproductive and child-care legislation. Done

28. Gain increasing control of your population. You can start this by controlling all immigration and visitation to your country. Then pick the minority group most feared or misunderstood by your followers and order a registration process. This will appear harmless, like getting a driver's license. Then incrementally increase the strength of this process, include more identifiable groupings, until all citizens must carry "papers" with them and submit to police checks. This will instill fear. In progress

29. Finally, incrementally increase your power and authority until you can accurately call yourself "president-for-life" or "Supreme Leader". This will take time. At some point you will need a crisis at home (Terrorist attack for e.g.) or you will need to provoke a crisis abroad and at home (Palestinian response to moving embassy to Jerusalem for e.g.). This will justify your transfer of a specific power from a democratic body (congress/senate/) to your own office. This can be done on the grounds that only you know all the facts, and quick decisions are required. It is also more acceptable if the democratic bodies are perceived as ineffective or too partisan. Your people can ensure the latter condition is met. Coming soon via N Korea or Iran.

— —-

Carl Jung spoke of Hitler embodying the collective unconscious of the German people. We needn't be as fanciful as Jung to see that a leader can personify and, by example, embolden the worst impulses of us humans, those impulses that may have had evolutionary utility when we fought over a watering hole and a hunting ground, those impulses that stand ready today to lead us down a dark path.

Las Vegas Massacre
Session 56

October 4, 2017

At any age there are some conditions (medical and other) that can befall us and cause aberrations in thinking and behavior. At age 64 they are unlikely to include the propaganda of ISIS or the illness schizophrenia or a drug induced psychosis. But they do include psychotic depression, brain tumour, frontal lobe dementia, and/or a combination of depression and early dementia. Psychotic depression refers to a combination of depression and paranoia.

When such a condition leads to violence it is usually isolated to suicide or murder-suicide. Even then the difference between suicide and murder/suicide (the murder usually being of a spouse) is often decided by the presence or absence of a lethal weapon.

An excellent available and affordable health and mental health system could catch some of these, institute treatment and prevent tragedy. But the simple solution to preventing 20 kids in a school or 59 people at a music festival from dying is gun control. Of course it's gun control. At least banning absolutely those kinds of weapons that can kill so many so easily.

I am writing this as professionals, journalists and armchair diagnosticians are all looking for a cause or motive for the recent mass shooting in Las Vegas. But my point is that such breakdowns, such dramatic (sometimes surprising, sometimes not surprising) changes in behaviour will always be with us. Sometimes an alert relative or family doctor can prevent a tragedy. But the difference between a single suicide or limited murder/suicide and mass casualties will always depend on available weapons.

I could make my guesses about what condition lay under Mr. Haddock's murderous actions and suicide but I shouldn't. For that is the wrong focus for any prevention of similar events in the future. If Americans, Congress and Senate are at all serious about preventing this kind of tragedy they need to forget trying to figure out what drove Mr.

120

Haddock and look instead at the insane ease which which he acquired his guns.

PLEASE NOTE: the name of the shooter used here is Haddock in order to illustrate just how unimportant that person's name is. The issue is gun violence and this article describes just how absurd the US emphasis on guns is https://www.vox.com/policy-and-politics/2017/10/2/16399418/us-gun-violence-statistics-maps-charts

More Assault on Democracy Session 57

October 16, 2017

In my list of instructions (the order was arbitrary) for undermining democracy, point 9 included curtailing unfavourable reporting by newspapers and TV networks via "licensing bodies". Donald Trump floated the idea in a tweet earlier this week, "at what point is it appropriate to challenge their license?" and then, apparently emboldened, directly suggested it a day later. "...licenses must be challenged and if appropriate, revoked..." His target this time is NBC.

The outrage has not been deafening. Perhaps because another Trump tweet suggested pulling FEMA out of Puerto Rico while accusing them of being in a financial mess of their own making, and he is about to sign a bill that will undermine the Affordable Care Act. He is also busy undermining multiple international agreements from NAFTA to UNESCO. And we are distracted by the crimes and misdemeanors of Harvey Weinstein and the killing spree of Mr. Paddock.

A serial killer inures himself to remnants of fear and anxiety by engaging in a self-designed desensitization process. The same process works with large populations. "This is an unusual presidency", someone says on CNN, "He doesn't fit the mold." "Should we take him literally?" "Should we take him seriously?" someone else asks.

But I think I have been most disturbed of late to hear even the thoughtful and presumably liberal experts and pundits on CNN tell me that, with respect to North Korea, "Diplomacy has failed. We have tried diplomacy for 25 years and it has failed."

And then even when they say war is not an option, they calculate the cost of war, conventional or otherwise, as being a few thousand U.S citizens residing in South Korea, perhaps a few million South Korean lives, and the devastation of the Korean peninsula.

So this is where we stand at the moment, 9 months in:

- Limit, by threat and licensing, the free press
- Create chaos and anxiety at home (the soil from which grows

tyranny)
- Vilify and dehumanize an enemy
- Desensitize the population to the truth and reality of war.

(in case anybody missed the point, North Korea has not attacked anyone in 25 years, so "diplomacy" has been working)

The Obama Legacy
Session 58

October 25, 2017

I have had a lifetime of sitting in a comfortable chair, walking safe streets, and observing the struggles of our neighbour to the south. Beneath their constant boasting I witnessed their progress, through Kennedy, desegregation, Johnson, Alabama, Martin Luther King, until finally they elected a black president. Which meant, I thought, that at least half of the population of the United States had worked through their demons of oppression and slavery, of segregation, of racism. Their future looked bright. And if the future of the USA looks bright so does that of the rest of the world.

But when I listen to Donald Trump, to Steve Bannon, to Harvey Weinstein for that matter, and many other white male Americans of age, I realize how much their terrible history is still in play. For beneath all of their bluster, their provocations, their aggression, there lies a deep pool of fear and guilt. Or guilt and then fear, which would be the correct order. Guilt to fear and then to aggression.

It is embodied by Donald Trump. It is being played out by Donald Trump on the world stage. His narcissism is astounding, as is his ability to lie, but he embodies another dynamic that must be addressed if the USA is not going to implode. And that is Donald's fixation on Barack Obama.

With much of what Trump says he leaves unspoken a final sentence that is beginning to ring loudly in my ears. And that is the removal of the "stain" of Barack Obama; the castration and lynching of Obama, expunging him from history.

The dynamic is guilt (guilt from deeds and thoughts and a denied history) which leads to a fear of retaliation, which is quickly turned into aggression.

It is risky applying individual psychology to the behaviour of groups and nations but over the past 50 years I think I have been watching Cognitive Behavioural Therapy being applied to America's history of

124

slavery, violence, segregation and racism. Superficially much progress has been made. "We shall overcome." But I think they need Desmond Tutu. Some truth and reconciliation. A full catharsis if we are not to see this cycle repeated again and again.

That is (and perhaps it will be possible in the backlash choice of president after Donald Trump), they need to really face their history, the truth of slavery, the remnants of the civil war, their guilt and fear. It could start with a loud and public discussion about all those civil war monuments and what to do with them.

After that they could look at the guilt they must feel for the destruction they unleashed on Vietnam, Cambodia, and Laos. Perhaps if that is ever faced we will no longer read that 50% of Republicans are in favour of a pre-emptive strike on North Korea.

Trump And/Or God?
Session 59

October 30, 2017

In Richard Russo's novel, "Nobody's Fool", Rub Squeers, sometime friend of Sully (played by Paul Newman in the movie), often says with a stutter, sometimes to Sully, sometimes to himself, "You know what I w-wish -t?"

His wish is usually for a small improvement in his circumstances, never realized. Yet, he is optimistic and quite endearing.

The moment science reported that those among us with a modicum of optimism live longer, recover faster from illness, and tolerate chronic illness better than pessimists, a poster went up in the hallway of a mental health center I visit, proclaiming HOPE in bold letters. It has since come down.

I thought of these things while watching a <u>bunch of religious</u> (or faith community) leaders praise Donald Trump and the power of prayer in the oval office. One went as far as to announce that we **all know prayer works**. They each thanked Donald within the same paragraph they thanked God, knowing, I'm sure, who really had the power to dispense favour at this moment.

Of all the players in these three separate stories I think I prefer the simple honesty of Rub Squeers. He wishes, and momentarily it gives him hope and small pleasure, but he has few expectations as he trundles on getting by.

And prayer itself. I have always had a problem with prayer. Okay, it can support hope; it can strengthen community, but this juxtaposition of the stroking of Trump's ego and the appeals to God certainly drew a clear parallel. For prayer itself implies that before God might notice my suffering, I must praise him. Not just praise him, but prostrate myself before him, beg him to intervene. So that image of God, that particular concept of God, involves an ego even bigger than Donald Trump's. God the narcissist.

And as long as they have prayer I suppose they can continue to pave

126

over the wetlands, ignore the disrepair of the damns, dykes, levees and drainage systems, cut taxes, remove environmental regulation, promote unfettered growth, and ignore climate change.

Trick or Trump Session 60

November 1, 2017

I had in my office yesterday an 11 year old who was in a bit of trouble at school. His defense was "Kevin did worse than me and he didn't get in trouble."

I laughed and then explained to the parents that I had just read a Donald Trump tweet along the same lines, "What about Crooked Hillary and the Dems."

The parents smiled warily, but the boy took offense. He did not like being compared to Donald Trump. I tried to explain that deflecting the blame, or trying to do that from an immature sense of playground fairness, was quite appropriate at his age. He was still unhappy that I had compared him to Donald Trump.

Then I saw a 12 year boy, a little fire-plug of a kid who happens to have a mop of blonde hair, a square face, and a passable rendition of a Donald Trump pout. I asked if he was going to go out Halloween as Donald Trump. No way he told me. There are too many Donald Trumps. He was dressing as a robber. Besides, Donald Trump is stupid.

So, at least, I concluded, the fear that Donald Trump might be a role model for our children, at least our Canadian children, is unfounded.

The Rise of the Far Right
Session 61

November 29, 2017

In the 1988 presidential debates Mike Dukakis was asked whether he would support the death penalty should his wife, Kitty, be raped and murdered. A long time opponent of the death penalty, Dukakis responded to the startling question from CNN's Bernard Shaw, "No, I don't, Bernard, and I think you know that I've opposed the death penalty during all of my life."

It struck me at the time that Dukakis missed a moment in which he could be human, present himself as fully human, and at the same time as worthy of being a president.

He could have answered, "Of course. If a man raped and murdered my wife I would want to disembowel him; I would want to kill him in a manner that caused him maximum pain and suffering. Which is exactly why we have laws, and courts, and due process. Which is exactly why it cannot be my choice as victim or survivor to decide in the heat of the moment what should happen to the accused or convicted. Which is exactly why, to remain a civilized people, we must decide on appropriate penalties that will keep us civilized, that will not harden or poison our souls, that will not undermine our social contract. If the state does not value life, why should its people?"

And herein lies a human dilemma. We are biologically not far removed from chimpanzees and great apes. Our instincts, our immediate emotional responses, have been honed for years as jungle tribes. We guard our own watering hole. We are reluctant to share. We distrust the other. We are greedy. We are vengeful. We are easily brought to rage.

But, at least since the second world war, with many attempts before then, we have managed to overlay our primate instincts with a social contract that includes the rule of law. We have elected many leaders who could see beyond their primate selves and form alliances, be inclusive, share watering holes. We have created international forums, unions, agreements. At least in much of Europe and North America.

But those primitive instincts remain, the ones that led to the Holocaust, the massacres in Bosnia, the plight of the Rohingya, the destruction of Syria, the building of walls. They lie not far beneath the surface of each human. It is our collective that can overcome them, and that collective must have leaders and lawmakers who can see beyond their immediate fears and desires. Leaders and lawmakers who appeal to our better selves.

We always have had would-be leaders who could reach in and stoke our fears, fire up our distrust and hatred, get us ready to pick up torches and weapons, defend our watering holes from thirsty strangers, set upon those unlike ourselves in our villages. But, for the most part we have rejected them and chosen instead the Merkels and the Obamas. Trade has flourished. Europe has seen a long period of peace, cooperation, and open borders. Overall the people of this planet live longer and healthier lives than ever before.

I am writing this because a cousin asked me to write about the current struggles in Austria, where a far right fascist party has gained enough support to become part of a coalition government. This is happening seventy-two years after the death of Adolf Hitler, 90 years after the early Nazi's received only 779 votes in a general election in Austria (1927), and 79 years since Nazi Germany annexed Austria.

I know little of the intricacies of Austrian life and politics. But this resurgence of the far right neo-fascist movement is occurring nearly everywhere in the west. Its leaders are appealing to our primate instincts, our rat brains. And this time, just as in the years between 1927 and 1938, they are finding more and more people responding to their simple message.

They stoke our fears and our grievances. Some of these are real. Most are manufactured or displaced. They point the finger at the other, the cause of our trouble. We respond and chant "Lock her up." "Build a wall." "Divorce Europe." "Stop Immigration."

We should have learned, especially Austrians, where this can lead. But apparently we didn't.

Neo-fascism, jingoism, isolation, the breaking of alliances, the undermining of cooperation and the weakening of our international institutions will not fix our problems. And from recent history we know exactly where this trend can lead.

Our instant access of unfiltered world wide information, some truth, some fake, has us grossly exaggerating our risk. We find ourselves afraid of events that have a miniscule chance of occurring. We fear a terrorist attack more than we fear riding a motorcycle, when clearly death by motorcycle is far more likely than death by terrorist. Donald Trump can make us fear illegal immigrants when that, statistically, should be the least of our worries.

We do have real problems, problems big enough to spell the end of a habitable earth.

Paradoxically, these real problems can only be addressed by the unified, cooperative, inclusive, citizenry of one planet. These real problems cannot be addressed by walled off, exclusive, defensive separate states, each populated by a homogenous group of humans who feel they are the chosen.

We are really all at risk because of an interrelated set of developments:

- Over population
- Extremely uneven wealth distribution
- Man-made global warming.
- And a large subset of problems that flows from these three.

We can change this, turn it around, make progress, but only if we can function as the citizenry of one world, only if we have strong international institutions, only if we recognize that we will survive together or perish alone.

Looking At Trump and Thankful for a Constitutional Monarchy Session 62

January 22, 2018

Mike Pence looks upon Donald Trump with besotted eyes. Six months after the election Trump can get a crowd chanting "Lock her up." I watch Jeffrey Lord, once an acolyte of Ronald Reagan, crawl through semantic swamps to throw himself at the feet of The Donald.

I read many accounts of how and why Donald Trump won that election: The forgotten citizens of the rust belt, of coal country and small town America. The rise of a populist leader sewing division, preying on our instinctive distrust of the other tribes who may covet our watering hole.

But I am also aware of very many successful cult leaders, men who can grow a following of thousands (or millions) in order to steal all the gold and the young women. To say nothing of tin pot dictators, cruel despots, and other false prophets.

It all speaks to a flaw in our human character, and a flaw, like many of our flaws, that once had survival value.

I'm sure when we lived in the jungles, even when we rode horseback on the prairies, and our tribes were beholden to a single alpha male, when we even sometimes thought of this alpha male king as a God king, we were stronger as a tribe when we offered blind allegiance, when we never questioned his decisions, and when we overlooked his indiscretions and malfeasance. Not that long ago we would shout "For King and country" as we rushed off to war.

This all implies an ability (a tendency) we have to project unto our leader, our king, the strongest of our desires and wishes, to assign to him the kinds of wisdom and compassion and strength that we would wish to see in our leaders, and in ourselves. We see such a leader, not

132

as he really is, but as we would want him to be. Donald was right when he said his base would still vote for him if he shot someone on Fifth Avenue.

With the checks and balances of the American Constitution, with the equally powerful House, Senate, Judiciary, and with the fourth estate intact, America may survive this despot and our very human tendency to see someone as we wish to see ourselves.

But I write this really as a plea to keep our constitutional monarchy in Canada. We humans need a King or Queen and a Royal Family, as long as they have no legislative power. Then we can project into them all that we wish to. We can revere them, talk about them, read the gossip and inside dope, admire their wealth and stateliness. We can argue about their usefulness and cost. We can enjoy the pomp and circumstance. They can be our symbols of power and goodness. They can be the embodiment of our collective.

And as long as we have a monarchy it will let us see Justin Trudeau as a guy doing a half decent job as a member of parliament and, for now, our Prime Minister. Fully human, entirely replaceable. Even though he made the cover of Rolling Stone, we will still listen to what he says and watch what he does, and judge him accordingly. And we and our parliament will hold him accountable for all that he says and all that he does.

Alternative Facts Session 63

February 14, 2018

I was probably ten or twelve when I asked my Sunday school teacher if there was any archeological evidence supporting the parting of the Red Sea and its collapse back over all those chariots. And in grade 7 when our science teacher, Mr. Edmonds, asked the class which way the earth travels around the sun and I told him it depends where in the universe the observer is standing. We argued and he sent me to see the Vice Principal from whom I first heard the idea of 'convention'.

And then we all run into professors in first and second year university who tell us of the social manufacture of reality, and those who tell us how our attitudes and perceptions are shaped by the power elite. And we run into G. E. Moore and Bertrand Russell and ponder the nature of truth. "Moore, are there apples in your basket?" And somewhere along the line a professor turns a chair upside down, places it on a table and asks the class, "What is this?" We tell him it is a chair, and he asks us how we know it is a chair. And someone else tells us that a light switch is neither on nor off, but in a position of relative on-ness, and that an electron might be in two places at once.

During his summer vacation between first and second year university, my grandson, in the comfort of his bedroom, day trades cryptocurrency on his new laptop. We discuss the nature of cryptocurrency, tulip bulbs, and "real" coinage, the very concept of money. I see that some articles on bitcoin are illustrated with a graphic of large, hard, embossed gold and silver coins. The irony is striking. The economists see bitcoin as a silly invented bubble; the bitcoin "experts" talk of cryptocurrency as being as big a social disrupter as the internet, liberating currency as the internet liberated information.

There are ads every night on CNN supporting legitimate journalism. They sometimes show an apple from first one angle and then a second and proclaim that it is still an apple. I think the ad writers missed the Beyond the Fringe parody of Russell and Moore, and Duchamp's painting of a pipe titled, "This in not a pipe."

"Moore, are there apples in your basket?"

And then we have Carter Page who apparently is referred to as a "Famous American Economist" when he gives talks in Russia, and Sean Hannity, and President Trump "totally vindicated" by the Nunes memo.

Many explanations for the rise of Donald Trump have been written, grounded in the history of the USA, the technological changes sweeping the world, the paranoia that accompanies mass migration, the always present racism, the forgotten but once privileged white working man, the attraction of populism and demagoguery....

And we are all fascinated by the extent this man can obfuscate, dissemble, lie, confabulate, and contradict himself without consequence.

But, pulling these random thoughts together, it seems to me that with Moore and Russell we left behind the certainty of 19th century truth, and with space travel, the origins of the universe, black holes, space time continuum, anti-matter, the digital revolution, the internet, robots doing our vacuuming and manufacturing, the democratization of information, the ubiquity of video illusion, virtual reality, artificial intelligence, and, perhaps most importantly, the development of every day tools that only a few really understand.....we are now a very bewildered species. We used to know where we were going. Now we don't. We used to understand our tools; now we don't. We are inundated with fiction; we binge watch Netflix. Many teen boys can recite the political intricacies of the Star Wars series much better than that of their own world. In our fictions there are an astonishing number of American Special forces whizzing around the world killing bad guys and keeping us safe. We find ourselves applying the expectations and conventions of fiction to reality. Conspiracies abound in fiction, though real humans are more prone to folly.

It has long been preached that truth will outlive a lie. But today that lie can be widely disseminated in seconds, with conviction and graphics, while the truth is often slow, difficult, and complex. Today the lie has done its job long before the truth emerges.

It is no wonder that many of us sitting in our puddle of bewilderment and angst are easily coaxed back to primitive religions, pre-enlightenment medicines, strong-men, demigods, and false prophets.

135

There is a heartening backlash to all this, symbolized in a small way by Georgian College throwing out its program in homeopathy. And in reality the economies of the world are all in better shape than they ever have been, fewer people starve, fewer people die of preventable and treatable illnesses (thanks to modern western medicine), more have access to clean water (modern medicine and science), fewer people are crippled or die from nutritional deficiencies (modern medical use of supplements and scientific dietary advice), fewer people are actually killing one another than ever before, fewer are enslaved, many with chronic illnesses have better lives..... We even have better and better treatments for mental illness...and I don't mean pig pills, micro-nutrients, and mindfulness.

We are at a tipping point I think. Can sufficient numbers of us, members of this human race, accept the reality of uncertainty, live with the angst of self-aware existence, discard the need for Gods and demigods, accept the scientific manner of seeking truth as primary, accept our species and ecological scientific truths, and get down to the task of preserving and expanding our democratic institutions, accepting this small planet as home to us all, and recognize we face two daunting tasks if we are to survive, that we must deal with over-population and global warming?

And this does not mean we should be wasting time and money shooting large rockets and small roadsters into Asteroid belts.

PS – David Stephan who was mentioned at length in the previous blog, went on a Facebook live video rant earlier this week attacking everyone involved in the cancellation of his lectures including Marvin Ross and Dr Terry Polevoy.

I feel left out. You rant against Marvin Ross and Terry Polevoy. Please add Dr. David Dawson to your list of trolls.

Now, two things: You and your wife were very scientific. You conducted an N of one experiment using nutrition, Pig Pills and supplements on a very ill child rather than taking him to a doctor for appropriate examination, tests and the application of modern medicine. The legal aspects of this are complicated. What is clear is that your pig pills and supplements and "Truehope" failed, and the child died. Your child died.

At the end of your diatribe on Facebook you say the "saddest thing" is the cancellation of your promotional speaking gigs. I would have thought it was the death of your child. It should have been the death of your child.

Arming Teachers Session 64

February 26, 2018

Samuel L Jackson put the issue quite succinctly:
"Can someone that's been in a Gunfight tell that Muthafukka that's Never been in a Gunfight, the flaws of his Arm The Teachers plan??!!"

Reading the comment section on any news item is usually not conducive to mental health or stress reduction. But, sometimes I read a few.

This one caught my eye in the middle of a discussion about the hapless deputy who "Waited behind a pillar for four minutes while the sound of semiautomatic gun fire rang through the school."

Somebody pointed out the deputy was armed with a handgun and going up against a killer with an AR 15 would be foolish. Then somebody else responded that:

"You'd be surprised how often a single handgun has taken out a nest of machine gunners."

And that was the comment that intrigued me. For there is only one place anyone could possibly see a man armed with a pistol "take out a nest of machine gunners" even once, let alone often, and that would be in fiction as portrayed on TV, Film and video.

We are watching slippage in those boundaries (reality, reality TV, Fiction) within the citizens, the politicians, and the President of the USA as they promote arming teachers.

They must be envisaging the kinds of shootouts that occur in NCIS LA and other shows every week: The heroes are fearless, often quipping when entering the battle. They are invisible to the bad guys. They shoot with pin point accuracy, from any position and distance. Their bullets never stray. They have invisible Kevlar vests. The bad guys are always easily identified. The bad guys are

138

always terrible shots, even with automatic weapons. Their bullets somehow move slowly enough for the good guys to duck. The bad guys conveniently step away from their cover to be shot. In the end the heroes walk away unscathed, not even emotionally distressed.

Mr. Trump. That is fiction. You are imagining Gary Cooper at High Noon, John Wayne, Stallone, your own adolescent fantasies.

The more guns firing, the more people get killed. The more guns carried the more likely an accidental shooting will occur. Or an unrelated homicide or suicide.

Steps in the Unraveling of a President Session 65

February 28, 2018

Some wondered if Donald Trump's latest tweet storm heralded an unraveling. This time he bounced back ˙with a somewhat adult response to gun control, in so far as raising the the age of legal purchase and banning "bump stocks" is at least a beginning. (He later returned to the NRA talking points of "hardening schools" and arming teachers)

So he didn't unravel completely but he certainly gave us intimations of things to come.

As the Mueller investigation grinds on with more and more indictments and guilty pleas what can we expect from Donald J. Trump?

A supreme narcissist, like a child when cornered or caught stealing or reprimanded will fall back on an **ever regressive series of deflections and denials**:

- It starts with straight denial. (never happened, wasn't me, fake news, hoax, didn't say that, I'm the most honest person you'll ever meet)

- Boasting about other things is added to this to distract and shore up his sense of omnipotence. "Popularity, security, number of bills passed, military budget." This is compared to the failing of sibs or, in this case, all previous presidents.

- It moves quickly to blaming someone else for the current problem, usually a brother or sister when a child. In this case Obama and Crooked Hillary, the Dems, the previous administration.

- Next comes a statement of unfairness or injustice. "You never get after my sister and she does worse things." "Obama was worse, how come he doesn't get in trouble? Look at what Hillary got away with? You should be looking into the Uranium deal?"

- And then accusations of unfairness, prejudice on the part of parents (FBI, Justice Department). "You never liked me. You always

140

liked Obama more than me. You gave Hillary a pass." You are terrible parents (Congress, FBI, Justice Department). I hate you.

- Then perhaps a string of unrelated accusations against a sister or brother or friend or teacher. In this case the Dems, various Senators, Obama, the Justice Department.

- And then the temper tantrum. The weeping, yelling, pounding of fists on the floor, stomping of feet. In this case a flow of whiny, semi-coherent profanities and mutterings. A mix of self-aggrandizement and self-pity.

- And then some lashing out.

And this is when more than the reputation and solvency of the USA is at risk. This is when we are all at risk.

Donald Trump is Helping My Psychiatry Practice – An Open Letter Session 66

March 5, 2018

Dear Donald from Dr David Laing Dawson

As much as I dislike your intrusion into my thoughts and my life several times every single day, Donald, I must say you are a gift to clinical work. No longer do I have to rely on obscure references, examples that may or may not be known to my patients; no longer do I need to dream up ice breakers to relax an anxious family; no longer do I need to struggle to find a topic that will provoke an emotional reaction in a silent, sullen teenager; no longer do I need to search for a way of introducing the topics of narcissism, empathy, sociopathy, and adolescent cognitive development.

Just today I asked a 17 year old how he thought he might react if he were outside the Florida school while the shooting was occurring. He thought for a few seconds and then said he would probably take cover and call the police. Seventeen Donald, and he has already outgrown that adolescent fantasy of yours you told the governors. Or at least he has reached a level of cognitive development when he understands those common male heroic rescue fantasies are just that, fantasies.

At what age does one still boast about these superhero fantasies? I suspect thirteen, fourteen maybe. And then, usually, a little more self awareness creeps in. I was able to congratulate my patient on being more thoughtful and mature than the President of the United States. He didn't think it was much of a compliment.

An anxious family, a parent with unruly or sullen child seeing a psychiatrist for the first time: I'm getting cautious one-word answers; I throw "Donald Trump" into this and the parents and the child all start talking with hand gestures, vivid facial expressions.

The mother tells me the 14 year old boy stole money from her purse. The boy launches into his defense, following the exact pattern of

Donald's tweets that very morning: Denial, fake news, someone else did it, you shouldn't leave your purse out, I don't get an allowance, my sister did it, you never blame her, she gets away with lots, you don't like me, you're unfair.

I point out the similarity. The mother smiles; the boy is insulted.

The teen girl over thinks everything. It is part of an OCD/anxiety problem. She is so worried and conscious of what she might say, and what she has said, that she avoids talking to all but family. I tell her I would like to inject her with a half ounce of Donald Trump. And there we have an extreme opposite to her problem that we can talk about.

The parents are very upset their child lies. I talk about lying, for a child, is natural, and how a developmental task for the child and teen, aided by their parents, is learning, by adulthood, when to lie or obfuscate a little bit, and when to tell the truth. At this age, the boy's lying does not mean he's going to grow into a Donald Trump or a career criminal.

It's a measure of severe depression when someone does not have the energy to become animated by the topic of Donald Trump.

It's a measure of excess idealism when a teenager is extremely distressed, outraged, horrified by the very mention of the name.

And there was a time when a fairly large percentage of teenagers, unable to answer any questions on current events, politics, governance, would explain, "It doesn't effect me; I'm not interested in it."

But they all now pay some attention to American Politics. They know your name and they all react. So there is one demographic the better for your existence: teens and youth. Let's hope they maintain their awareness and idealism.

143

A Porn Star May Be Our Last Hope Session 67

March 19, 2018

The Vatican's secretary of state, Cardinal Eugenio Pacelli (the future Pope Pius XII), and Germany's vice chancellor, Franz von Papen, formally signed a concordat between the Holy See and the German Reich on July 20, 1933.

Hitler had been appointed Chancellor in January of that year.

But this Concordat was just one of the incremental events that opened the door for a criminal dictatorship to evolve and unleash the worst of human potentials.

Trump is not Hitler. Hitler harboured some extreme ideologies and hatreds from the beginning. Trump's ideology is Trump. America in 2018 is not Germany in 1933. But, like Hitler, Trump is systematically undermining the safeguards of democracy.

Today Trump does not need an agreement with the Vatican to stay away from politics. But he does need, just as Hitler needed Papen, the generals, and the aristocrats – he does need the leaders of the Republican party to treat him like a useful idiot, to faun over him, to excuse him, to believe they are merely using him to achieve their own goals and maintain their power.

Trump has rendered the fourth estate powerless. Any one of their reported scandals and satires might have unseated a politician years ago. But today it all feels like a reality TV show, and thus more entertaining than consequential.

So we are left with an independent judiciary and independent law enforcement. But now it appears we are entering the end game.

I have described Trump as mentally and emotionally about 14. He says he is a "stable genius". I would dispute the "stable" qualifier, but he just might be a genius, an evil genius, an evil genius with the emotional stability, cognitive apparatus, and vocabulary of a 14 year old. His methods, be they accidental or planned, of commanding the news cycles, provoking others to do his dirty work, testing the waters

("Maybe we should kill the drug dealers"), sewing the seeds of distraction, sewing rumours, bold lies repeated and repeated, and first killing off the ground support of any major impediment – this may be narcissistic and sociopathic, but it is clever.

And now, one of his few major obstacles is Mueller. Nunes, Fox and Friends have been kicking at Mueller's shins. And now Trump, unfettered, is attacking him directly. There is talk of a "constitutional crisis" if Mueller is fired. But it seems to me it will only be a crisis if the Republican party and the judiciary object.

Our last hope may be Stormy Daniels. God speed Stormy, bring this monster down.

Two Short Pieces – Trump Post Mother's Day Session 68

May 14, 2018

The United Banana Emirates

When Donald J. Trump brought his son-in-law and his daughter into the White House and gave young Jared something like 5 portfolios, 5 jobs to do, each requiring a full time employee with years of expertise and experience, pundits talked of despots, kingdoms, banana republics and nepotism.

Of course Jared could not do all those jobs, which may have been the point.

Then Mar a Lago became a "Southern White House", which meant important meetings and government business was being conducted in the potentate's country estate. There was surprisingly little outcry about this, but it struck me as an important step toward despotism. The president was no longer conducting business from the house of the people, but from his own castle. When the president of Japan visits it is not to the historic house of democracy, but to the wealth and splendour of the King's castle.

And now two more revelations about the drift to banana status: The President's personal lawyer, a Michael Cohen, has been selling access to the president for hundreds of thousands of dollars, and the very agencies established to protect the citizens and the planet from the excesses, from the greed and corruption of various industries, are now firmly under the control of those industries. That's Banana Republic 101.

Donald and the ethics of a psychiatric diagnosis

As a physician I should not diagnose, or label, a set of personality traits unless I do it to benefit my patient, to help him or her in some way. But Donald, you do have a narcissistic personality disorder. And knowing this can help you in the following way: You want to be revered, liked, loved at all times, congratulated, fawned over. You love to take credit for all good things that happen. You must undercut all competition for affection of others. Because of this disorder you can never be fully content. Your ego must be fed again and again.

And there are many who do express their love for you, who will applaud you, defend you, do your bidding without question, fawn over you. And you in turn will shower them with praise, affection, opportunity and money. But Donald, they don't love you, not really. They are almost as narcissistic as you are. They are just men (and a few women) who will sell their souls for a little second hand limelight, celebrity status, money, and the illusion of power.

You've given Giuliani, like an old opera star, a second chance on the stage. You've given Pruitt an opportunity to hob nob with the hoi polloi and get rich in the process. For Bannon and Putin you have been a useful idiot. You have given Cohen a chance to smoke cigars, swagger, make deals and get rich without doing much work. And the list goes on.

The point is, Donald, they don't really love you. Your narcissism renders you vulnerable to praise. And when your ship is sinking they will not be sharing their life vests with you.

The Erosion of American Democracy Session 69

June 6, 2018

From 1934 until the end of WWII the Nazi party passed over 40 incremental laws restricting Jewish presence and participation, leading inexorably to "the final solution". This is a desensitization process; each seemingly benign step leading to the next slightly less benign step.

In a previous blog, somewhat flippantly, I wrote out a do-it-yourself manual for the erosion and destruction of an established democracy. To a surprising degree much has already come about in the USA under Trump and the Republican Party in a mere 18 months.

Several recent events have pushed this timeline dramatically along.

Trump has quite unnecessarily pardoned Dinesh D'Souza as a message to Comey, Mueller and Rosenstein, and undoubtedly to Flynn and Cohen, demonstrating his power to the men who prosecuted D'Souza in the first place, and his support to those currently charged.

Then in a tweet he threw Manafort under the bus in a clear statement to the others that there are conditions attached to his promise of support and future pardon.

In the midst of this his lawyers sent a letter to Mueller suggesting or stating that The President cannot be charged and indicted for anything because ultimately this same man can decide what is illegal and what is not.

(I gather the idea that the President is not above the law is not that clearly spelled out in the constitution).

This notion should be shocking, but instead I hear it discussed, argued over, with talk of precedence and norms rather than disbelief, horror and immediate action.

Each of these steps are akin to the Nazi rulings. Desensitization is occurring.

I suggested a war with Iran or Korea would be necessary for Trump to enact some emergency measures in his waddle to dictatorship, but his instincts may be more clever than mine. For he seems to be ignoring

Iran now, and cozying up to North Korea, while starting a trade war with his allies. His use of "national security" as a pretext for the imposition of tariffs is telling. Maybe he does not need a real war. Perhaps he only needs a trade war with Europe, Canada and Mexico, with each of these allies retaliating in a way that hurts his base. In such a trade war the American people will feel more and more surrounded by enemies, a fortress besieged, alone in this fight with the world.

And that is when people are willing to turn to a charismatic leader who promises them everything – safety, security, prosperity, greatness – in return for a little blindness.

The clock is ticking my American friends.

What We Need to do to Survive Session 70

June 25, 2018

The DNA imperatives that propelled our species this far are someday going to kill us all. We seek patterns, linkages, cause and effect. Our brains organize our multiple visual and auditory experiences. Our brains are, as others have said, organizing machines.

Most other creatures have built in templates seeking a match: the pathway to food, to shelter, to procreation, to touch and comfort. Our dominance has been upheld by our brains' ability to organize information into new patterns, unique patterns, new cause and effect linkages, new explanations of cause and effect.

Galileo muttered, "And yet it moves" as he left the inquisition. Elon Musk says we need to colonize Mars. The Flat Earth Society is meeting in Saskatchewan (which is a good choice it occurs to me). Each brain is responding to the same imperative. The first has organized new information to arrive at a conclusion the church is not ready to accept. The second imagines a future from his own larger-than-life experiences and resources. The third clings to an old explanation by ignoring a wealth of other information.

A friend says, "They are both Leos; that explains it." He smiles, letting me know he is not wholly committed to that (demonstrably silly) template of understanding.

The delusional man tells me a song on the radio is about him, for him, a message only to him, written for him, played for him. His penetrating gaze tells me this is how he organizes information. He is a believer. He is psychotic.

Today my Google list of top news topics includes Xi Jinping, Doug Ford, Donald Trump, and Steve Bannon.

I know why Xi Jinping and Doug Ford are there. I will resist using the juxtaposition of those four names to draw any organizational conclusions about the world and it's future.

But Steve Bannon? Why is Steve Bannon back on the list?

And it turns out he is busy. Busy in Europe, especially Italy, meeting with numerous Populist Leaders, Far Right politicians, giving speeches, promoting…. I'm not sure what he's promoting actually. "History is with us," he says. He seems to be promoting the kinds of xenophobic, racist, exclusive, fascist, isolated enclaves that brought us both the First and the Second World War. He gathers information through his own filters and sees an apocalypse in our near future, a Fourth turning, a war of civilizations. The elitists can't win this war for us, he says. He promotes a populist movement fueled by Social Media, by reinventions of Briebart News. He seems to relish an age of warring tribes, this time with modern weaponry.

But where does he picture himself in this? Surely not as a robed and besieged emperor. Not as a Mussolini. Perhaps as the Consigliere who can escape to Argentina after the conflagration?

Bannon's grandiosity would not be important if he didn't have an audience. And that is the puzzle. Why are these people including Steve Bannon as a source of information to help them formulate their understanding of the world? Though I suppose they are simply selecting those who come with ideas that support the self-serving conclusions they already share.

To survive the ant must organize a pattern, a trail, that will lead him from the nest and back in search of food. And then the ant will stick with it. If I plant my shoe in that track the ant will ignore the bodies and simply go over that shoe.

To survive now we humans must, somehow, quell the need for simple, absolute patterns, the need that opens the door to the veneration of Imams and Popes and Kings and Presidents-for-life, and the Trumps, Bannons, and Fords of this world. And we need to overcome that genetic impulse calling us back to small, exclusive, warring tribes.

We humans have the gift of imagining new patterns; though, like the ant, we cling to the old. To survive, contrary to the impulses of Trump, Bannon, Miller, and many others, we need to imagine our tribes as more and more inclusive, less and less competitive, more and more cooperative.

151

On Shoes and the United States Space Force Session 71

June 27, 2018

He is so 14, our Donald. That is the 14 year old brain at work. He hears something, a story, and immediately propagates this as a truth that explains the world, or a part of it. Without judgement, context, history, accuracy, consideration.

Canadians have been smuggling shoes across the border. Clearly evidence of Canada's unfair punishing tariffs.

This is the level of reasoning I see clinically between age 12 and 14. After 14, usually, some questions, context, history, some sense of scale creep in.

Next we have the "Space Force" (cue the theme music; design the Star Trek costumes). "Warp speed ahead, Mr. Spock". The last time this made sense to anyone would be age 14. It is in late childhood and early teen years that we can emerge from a Sci Fi film and imagine what we have seen being a mere 10 years away.

I don't mean the computers, the communication devices, some of the clever prognostications sci-fi writers slip into their stories – I mean the whole thing – zipping around the universe in million ton craft and little dune buggies at warp speed in sexy uniforms. That's where the Donald's head is. And he would be, of course, Supreme Commander of, cue the music, The United States of America Space Force.

And all the lying and exaggerations. That is age 14. I very seldom, in clinical practice, see a teen alone. I always include the parent(s). I explain that, (exaggerating but a whit) without the parents in the room, it can take me a full hour to determine if the child in question is actually attending school. At 14 and 15 from the teen talk of "basically" and "pretty much" and "yeah, sure" to out-right avoidance and lying, I might, by the end of an hour, have his attendance nailed down to: 2 or 3 days per week does actually get to school by 8:30, vapes at the smoking pit, goes in the school but avoids classes, then leaves at noon.

We need responsible adults in the room. Both in my office and in the Oval office.

When is it Too Late? Or is it? Session 72

July 2, 2018

When the steps are incremental and desensitizing, inuring, it is difficult to know when we have moved beyond the point of no return. Many of us thought the separation of children from their parents and the incarceration of over two thousand children in cages all over the country might be a step too far and too fast. But even this is being obscured and overwhelmed with rhetoric and confusion, with Orwellian language.

And speaking of Orwellian language I notice that Trump is not bothering to use a full phrase in his accusations, such as accusing any number of democrats of being "soft on crime" or wanting "weak immigration policies". He has taken the next step in simplifying and labeling: The Democrats are "for crime", they are "for gangs", and they want "no borders."

"Power corrupts" is not an empty phrase. It is an observation of all human behaviour. From studies of our history to the guard/prisoner experiments of the 1960's. The gentlest person can find his or her inner tyrant when placed in the social context of supervising the weak and helpless. A few will wrestle with these unwanted impulses. Many will give into them.

I mention this because I detect a subtle shift in tone coming from the President of the United States. He is still prickly and defensive. He still manages to bring every issue back to himself and his greatness. He still denigrates Obama and all previous leaders to enhance his own reputation. (and to fuel the racism of his base)

But now his rallies and tweets have adopted a demagogic tone more directly and specifically. More and more his words place him above the law. More and more his words place him as the only important decision maker. More and more he ignores ethics and due process. More and more he aligns with tyrants and disparages the leaders of the democracies of this world with the worst derogatory word a mob boss

154

can muster: "weak".

His over-the-top rhetoric about the "Witch Hunt" is working. He is swaying public opinion. Most Republican politicians are falling in line. He may know little of history, compassion, governance, but he sure knows Goebbels ("If you tell a lie often enough...") and the principles of modern marketing.

He once added qualifiers to his outrageous lies and hyperbole. "They are rapists and murderers – though some I suppose are good people." He doesn't bother now. Immigrants are "invaders" and "infections". One step away from vermin and cockroaches.

Increasingly he directly threatens individuals and corporations in his tweets.

If we are not at the tipping point, my American friends, we are close.

Advice to the Donald on How to Keep Track of Seized Kids Session 73

July 11, 2018

Dear Donald,

It has come to my attention that you are having trouble reuniting the 2000 to 3000 apprehended children with their parents. It seems you may have to resort to DNA testing to determine who belongs with whom. (By the way, if you are worried that some might have been brought to the USA by sex traffickers you could simply ask them.)

Meanwhile, should you institute another roundup of children in the future might I recommend that you use a highly successful method of keeping track of them once used in an earlier roundup:

Simply tattoo a unique number on the arm of each child. Enter this number in a ledger along with the name and age of the child and the name of his or her parent. The forearm is a logical body part for such tattoos because it could accommodate a long number without resorting to an alphanumeric system. I will include a photo as a visual aid.

Please do not hesitate to call for further advice.

Sincerely,

Trump-Speak explained
Session 74

July 16, 2018

Listening to Donald Trump at any time is not conducive to equanimity but I clicked on the link to his "take on Brexit". He was asked about Brexit by a reporter as he stood behind a podium. At first, in a congenial way, he responded that he had been reading a lot about Brexit in anticipation of his upcoming visit to the UK. And then he elaborated in his usual style.

But I am writing about this because it was a clear demonstration of how Donald Trump's mind works, and of the concept of "associations".

When we listen to someone else, or to our own thoughts as we form sentences and speak words, each noun, verb, adverb and adjective can cause us to experience associations from other memories and experiences.

In a serious discussion about roses the word "pink" might be used, causing us to think of a "pink Cadillac" or the singer "Pink", but being in the context of a serious discussion about horticulture we will not let our brains and mouths take us off the topic at hand.

Now people with Asperger's or "on the ASD spectrum", not being as keenly aware of the intent of the speaker as others usually are, will often go off on an extraneous tangent, caused by a word association. Often it is a metaphor or simile mistaken for a factual statement of equal or more importance than the original topic.

Someone in a state of disorganized psychosis may appear to go off on an irrelevant tangent linked to a single word, and in that tangent the unusual linkages can occur over and over and may cause a "word salad.". "Word salad" being an extreme form of "loosened associations." Of course some of the associations may be to unspoken thoughts and feelings, including delusions and hallucinations.

With the toxicity of drugs, alcohol, infections, chemicals, the fractured sentence structure can be further impaired by problems of working, immediate, and recent memory and the distractions of distorted perceptions.

In dementia, with impairment of recent memory, the brain may associate words spoken, not with the forgotten recent topic, but with other older memories.

And, of course, with some people, the assault on linear, logical and cohesive sentence structure can come from word associations to an overwhelming theme, or trait, or need, or obsession. And here we have Donald Trump. Always, always to his own accomplishments, his self-aggrandizement, his prickly defensiveness, his greatness, his popularity, his wealth.

It is difficult to discern from his answer how much he actually knows about Brexit (probably very little). But the word "Ireland" took him to the properties he owns in Ireland, to how much they love him there, and on to the "magical" property he owns in Scotland, the birthplace of his mother, and the fact he owns properties "all over", but the people voted to leave the EU, and there will be protests, there will always be protests, and the word protests took him to his own experience of protests during his election (actually switching to the American election without naming it) and how many electoral votes he got, and the words won and election, took him to Wisconsin which he won and Ronald Reagan didn't win even when Reagan "swept the board".

There was nothing new here, but a clear demonstration of how much Donald Trump's narcissism intrudes and distracts from any cohesive linear thought about something other than himself.

In a similar vein, if one listens carefully to Trump's semantics, his choice of references, his associative processes, when he talks about the upcoming meeting with Putin, his narcissism prevents him from seeing himself as anything but himself, not as a representative of a country. His mind loops within the small circle of how he personally will be perceived and received by Putin (compared to all the lesser presidents who came before him of course).

In a sane world this man would now be making decisions about nothing more than the hair and tanning products he applies each morning. And perhaps what club to use on the dogleg seventh.

Delusional Narcissism and the Donald Session 75

July 25, 2018

It is time to make a prediction, though, as a relatively sane person, I know we can never be one hundred percent sure of anything. Seldom over 70% for that matter.

But here it is:

Donald Trump's pathology is becoming more and more evident in his off the prompter remarks, his lies and contradictions, his fractured adolescent English and his tweets.

If this simply continues, if the Republicans retain control of House and Senate, and Donald's popularity does not drop precipitously within his base, then step by step, under cover of the Trump circus, the Trump distraction, America will become worse in all ways. Let me list some of them:

Racial intolerance, racial strife
Women's reproductive rights, women's equality, gone
Fascist application of laws
Good health care for fewer and fewer.
Distribution of Wealth even worse
Destruction of the environment
Increasing corruption.
Larger and larger debt
More and more poor and black in prisons
Fewer, poorer welfare programs
Poorer public education
More tribal isolation
More gun violence
Damaged reputation in the rest of the world.

(And the world will suffer because we need a sane and healthy America)

On the other hand Mueller may indict Trump and/or members of his family and inner circle, or we find the Russians do have something on

159

him, or he fires Mueller and sets in motion a constitutional crisis. Whichever way Trump's presidency comes to an end the problem remains his narcissism.

Each of us may suffer a narcissistic injury from time to time. (a rejection, a loss, a failure, a disappointment). The healthiest among us nurse our wounds, learn from the experience, and become kinder, gentler, more thoughtful people. The more narcissistic flail longer, hurt more, deny longer, blame others, before they give in and learn from the experience. With a little more narcissism they remain hurt for longer, and may develop unhealthy coping mechanisms, such as continuing the blame, seeking revenge, obsessing.

And then we have the supreme narcissist. Usually such a person will organize his or her world to be immune from challenge. Which is perhaps where Donald Trump would be if he hadn't entered politics – surrounded by sycophants who support his illusion, be king of the resorts and golf courses he owns, print his name in bigger and bigger gold letters, make claims without challenge of being a stable genius who has written many books, and get his name in the news media as often as the Kardashians.

It was quite telling to hear Donald disrespect his own country at the Helsinki meeting. Some called this treasonous. But I think the explanation for this behaviour comes not just from his need to please Putin, but from his narcissism. By that I mean that another president would know that his or her power and status derived in fact from being the elected representative of the Country America and all it's institutions. Not Trump. His sense of his greatness precedes and exceeds his conferred status as President. He is "Trump". (the pun in this is one of those quirks of history)

And that level of delusional narcissism does not suffer injury lightly. He will flail and explode in rage. He will disorganize. He will blame and obsess. He will not go quiet into that good night.

The Tiff with Saudi Arabia
Session 76

August 8, 2018

Usually in our relations with nation states that have poor human rights records, Canada officially protests in polite fashion, the offending state responds in some grumbling way, and life goes on. Strategic, political alliances, and economic forces trump the rights of minority religions, journalists, little girls and women. Fair enough. Canada is not in a position to do much more than raise the issue anyway, and continuing to be engaged may be the most productive thing we can do in most cases.

Those fifteen thousand Saudi students in Canada just might take some civilized values back to the Middle East. Or not.

But we now have an opportunity to go beyond that. The over-the-top school-yard reaction by the Saudis, complete with a jpeg showing an airliner heading for the CN Tower, cancelling the scholarships of those 15,000 students, cancelling all future business deals, and sending our ambassador home, actually allows us now to be a little more direct and specific, without worrying about geopolitics and economics.

Saudi Arabia is a slave state. The girls and women of Saudi Arabia have only marginally more rights and dignity than a "house nigga" in 1840's Georgia. In fact, researching this it seems the only real difference may be the amount of leisure time and purchasing power afforded the Saudi women by the oil wealth of many households.

So, Chrystia and Justin. Opportunity knocks. Make it clear what you think of the enslavement of women, the absence of free speech, the control of the press, and their medieval system of justice.

As far as I can see, we need no longer be constrained by the strategic alliance between the USA and Saudi Arabia. In fact, it is Donald Trump who has emboldened the dictators and potentates of this world. He will no doubt say something like, "There are good people on both sides", or even favor the Saudis over Canada in this dispute.

While we watch the craziness south of our border unfold, we must remain independent and give clear voice to our liberal democratic principals.

162

Pennsylvania and the Catholic Church Session 77

August 22, 2018

A cult is a cult is a cult is a cult.

The Cathedral at Chartres, I suppose because of its magnificence as well as its age and physical location, allows one, as I did, to stand in it and outside it and imagine the 14th century: the fields stretching off in the distance, the peasants on foot and oxen cart slowly approaching this edifice, dressed in rough cloth tunics and hand sewn goat skin boots, bringing what offerings they could. This cathedral was built to impress, and impressive it is. And that I suppose is its purpose. It is, in modern vernacular, awesome, and in the centuries before this, designed to instill awe.

Standing there it is easy to imagine those illiterate peasants approaching the castle of knowledge and salvation. They did not yet understand why there was night and day or why water ran downhill or some fell ill with fever and others didn't. And the church, for the next few centuries, would try to keep it that way.

And at Chartres, more than other cathedrals and churches, it is easy to see and experience the power of the building, and to understand its purpose by imagining the first hundred years of its existence.

Power and control. And, more quietly of course, sex.

What a con. What a magnificent con.

I'm not really knocking it, for we humans seemed to need an organizing system and some guiding principals sent to us from on high. Even now, in parts of the world where we have socially evolved to the point where we can, through very human processes, set those rules and expectations ourselves, many of us still yearn for the help of God. And, God knows, the Catholic Church, for much of its existence, has been no worse than Islam, Scientology, Mormonism, the Peoples Temple Agricultural Project, or the Branch Davidians.

163

But I would like to point out that it is we humans who have, **within our own secular governing bodies**, in many parts of the world, arrived at the conviction that a.) women are full citizens with equal rights, b.) men do not have the right to non-consensual sex with women, and c.) we adults really shouldn't be sexually abusing children and teenagers. Note that it is not Joseph Smith, the Pope, the Imams of Saudi Arabia, or Jim Jones who arrived at those conclusions.

Cults. It is what they are all about of course. They strip women of power. They permit non-consensual sex or, at the very least, coercive sex with females. And they justify the sexual abuse of children, pre or post pubertal children, male and female. And they all prey on the innocence and naivety of our less educated, less wary and less suspicious citizens. They are all, all, all about power, control, and sex.

Someone pointed out that if it had come to light that over 300 Jiffy Lube employees had been discovered to have sexually abused over 1000 children it would be the end of Jiffy Lube, but the Catholic Church will continue, as will Islam, and it seems there are always a few charismatic psychopaths (male) hanging around ready to start new cults.

Though it has been heartening to see, over the past 50 years, that increasingly large percentages of the citizens of most advanced nations, when polled, say they are either not religious, or do not belong to any particular religious group or cult.

Trying to Explain Qanon
Session 78

September 7, 2018

I fell down the internet rabbit hole today, after reading about QANON followers, supporters, supplicants at the Trump rally in Florida. Apparently this is pronounced Cue Anon and it refers to a source, a guru, a (supposed) government leaker, a group espousing a number of deep state conspiracy theories.

And following this path into the corners of the internet I came across word salads of meaningless connections the likes of which I have only seen before with psychosis, specifically schizophrenia.

As if global warming and the rise of right wing populists were not enough to worry about we now have a rising tide of people espousing and broadcasting delusions.

I have written before that delusions are never about trivial matters, but always about the central vectors of existence in our social world: Power, Sex, Control, Worth. And, curiously, QANON manages to conflate all of these. (Deep state control of our lives along with sex trafficking and pedophilia)

And what does this mean?

The brain is an organizing machine. It seeks cause and effect, linkages, symbols, connections. The sane mind in a relatively well organized society will find **mostly** the same linkages as everyone else and these linkages will be both plausible and possible; they will connect within the same physical and temporal spheres, and will support safety and success. They allow us to predict what will happen next.

When the brain is impaired, when it's perceptual, filtering, and organizational apparatus are impaired, it will continue to make linkages and some of these may be crazy. That is, they may jump from one physical or temporal sphere to another. (e.g. an earthquake in Peru was caused by the bad thoughts I had yesterday, or 4 blue cars drove by and Donald Trump used the word "four" and there are four somethings in the bible, therefore...) Similarly when we cut off all input (sensory deprivation experiments and solitary confinement) the brain continues to form linkages, find cause and effect paradigms, and these may then (unhindered by solid external data) become fantastical.

The QANON people can't all suffer from impaired brains, nor are they sensory deprived. That leaves the possibility that the same effect that illness (like schizophrenia) and/or sensory deprivation can have on the brain can also be caused by extreme internet information overload and social persuasion. Though I would have to assume that this overwhelming information load only disrupts the cognitive patterns of those that lack a solid foundation of meaning and understanding, that is, a way of organizing information within the same temporal and physical spheres of reality and plausibility. For just as with delusional schizophrenia, a single visual mark, a symbol, or a nonspecific sound, can, in Qanon minds, leap categories and time constraints and become a theory of everything. They write, podcast, and talk as if a hundred miniature Dan Browns resided in their frontal lobes leaving Illuminati parchment clues to pizza parlor Clinton sex trafficking, illegal immigrants, Jews, Muslims, Hollywood pedophiles, and the apocalypse. Not to forget the Elite and the Deep State. This is not conspiracy theory. This is delusional.

There is another slightly more benign explanation, and that is that our entertainment world, including reality TV, has grown so pervasive and persuasive that more and more people can no longer tell the difference, and/or find fiction just more interesting and fun than reality.

In the long run solid public education is probably the answer, and we need to teach our kids and teens how to organize, to learn, to categorize, to think scientifically and logically.

In the short run, unfortunately, I can see groups like Qanon becoming Donald Trump's Brown Shirt enforcers.

Article 25 of the US Constitution Session 79

September 10, 2018

Many pundits have referred to Trump as a Reality TV President, partly referring to the origins of his infamy, and partly to the way he operates as a politician and leader. But the description is increasingly apt. The whole scene – the White House, daily tweets, the books, the anonymous op ed, the daily coverage and panel discussions, the leaks – it has all taken on the tone of Reality TV. And as it takes on this tone – the vying for limelight, the petty competitions, grievances aired, boasting, lying, the focus entirely subjective, the absence of actual reality, the absence of awareness of a world beyond the bubble – we fall into watching it the same way. Each day we tune in to watch these conflicts unfold, and just as in Reality TV, we are far more concerned with the relationships of all involved than with the prize (in Realty TV) and the enacted policies (in governance). Our hunger for prurient detail, for the personality machinations, conflicts, buffoonery, stupidity and chicanery in and surrounding Trump overwhelm our concern for health care, international relations, and global conflict.

In Reality TV the conceits of drama are imposed in the editing room. Here they are imposed by the Media, the watchers, the Late Night Hosts, and Trump himself.

I am thinking of this as I wonder how the Trump presidency will end. Last night he told his supporters that if he is impeached he will hold them responsible for not voting in the midterms.

If the Democrats do regain control of Senate and Congress and start impeachment proceedings, what will happen? How will Trump behave?

We know he will not go quiet (or gentle) into that good night. We know, at least as far as I can see, that his profound narcissism never ever permits a breach in his defenses, an admission of failure or of being bested in some way. We know this is extreme. We know that he will take praise and support from anyone, including Kim Jong Un. We know he is capable of seeing what he wants to see, to a delusional degree. And we know, unfortunately, that he is not constrained by a conscience, by empathy for others. And we know that people who lie to others as easily as he does, also lie to themselves.

We also know he will rage and blame others and that he is capable of outrageous lies to support his position.

If this were Shakespeare we could leave him in the turret of his castle railing at the moon.

But will he sabotage the castle when he is cornered? Will he burn Paris as he retreats?

Unfortunately I think the answer to that question is YES.

So if the Democrats gain power and start impeachment proceedings I think they need to be prepared to invoke Article (Amendment) 25 before Donald J. Trump lights the match.

Doug Ford, Donald Trump Session 80

September 13, 2018

I just heard Doug Ford proclaim that he was elected by 2.3 million people whereas the judge was appointed by one person.

This is perilously close to a Trumpism.

Our systems of governance are complicated and cumbersome. Our judiciary is independent and equally complicated and layered. They have evolved this way not so that one man or woman can easily get things done but to prevent one man or woman or a group of men and women from doing stupid harmful things. From the moment I became aware of governance and politics, as far as I can remember, Canadian and American politicians, presidents, premiers, prime ministers understood this – up until the last 2 years.

Donald J. Trump demonstrates every day that he does not understand this. He has had 72 plus two hundred years to learn. He didn't. And it seems a portion of the American population have forgotten as well. And another portion of the American population has become inured.

And now this is creeping into Ontario. We seem to have a Premier with Donald Trump instincts, the instincts of a bully, of an anti-democratic strongman. And like Donald Trump, he is willing to trample on democratic principles to push through his own agenda, both, tellingly, the small, personal and petty as well as serious policy.

The number of Councilors representing parts of the biggest city in Canada is not an important issue. It can be adjusted with discussion, consultation, voting, over time as demographics and population densities change.

It is an historical pet grievance of one Doug Ford. To use the "not withstanding clause" of the charter to override a judicial decision about such an arbitrary unimportant issue is stupid, reckless, thoughtless. And this is not about good governance of Toronto or Ontario. It is about the fragile ego of one Douglas Ford.

Please let us not follow the Americans down that regressive path.

Trump and the Y2 backlash
Session 81

September 17, 2018

As the year 2000 approached I wondered about backlash. There was, as you will recall, that unfounded fear of computer disruption, but I thought this magic number might be seen as symbolic of our new realities. And might not the people of this world who live within a pre-science, pre-knowledge bubble need to rebel against the onslaught of scientific information and truth? Won't they need to recoil from this new millennium?

At the time I was thinking about those who hold medieval religious beliefs, of whatever flavour. How will they cope? How will they cope with the unavoidable (thanks to the internet) knowledge of our world from subatomic particle to an expanding universe, from the origins of life on earth to evolution and the human brain?

We got a taste of this, I think, with the rise of Islamic Extremists and their propagation of a way of life (and level of knowledge) my ancestors left behind shortly after the year 1000, or at least by 1700.

The Christian fundamentalists took a more nuanced approach concocting alternatives to evolution, modern medicine and quantum mechanics. (I just read a very bizarre conflation of biblical symbolism and the function of the human brain, most notably the pineal and pituitary gland, which, I did not know, are referenced in the bible as Joseph and Mary and who send some kind of oil down the spinal cord to the manger....but you get the drift).

Some Asian and Indigenous belief systems have been more easily adapted to this new age and the possibility there just might be some unseen forces we have not yet been able to detect and measure, and the fact there really is an almost magical ecological inter-connectedness between all living things. Even some trees "communicate" one to another when under threat of pestilence.

Though it is a surprise to see "alternative" medicine flourish, and people believing in unseen energy pathways running through the body from the big toe to the frontal lobe and which can be disrupted by a needle inserted according to a chart drawn up before we even knew about nerves and blood vessels, hormones and bacteria.

But a bigger surprise are the large numbers of people who are responding to Donald Trump and the other populist leaders. But then, of course, that is the real backlash, the recoil.

It is not just the religious fundamentalists our world is leaving behind, it is great masses of people who pine for 1950 (perhaps an imagined 1950) and a world of known order and expectation, a world of homogeneity, a world in which we feel we have some control and a bright future, a world without the daily intrusion of others, a world in fact where we don't have to spend much time thinking about others, a world in which we don't have to be frightened every day by dying tropical reefs, rising oceans, and Ebola outbreaks in Africa. A world in which most of us have at least a basic understanding of the tools we use. A world where we don't ever have to think hard about our history, our heroes, our place in the universe.

That is the world Donald Trump is promising Americans. And wouldn't it be nice: Pre-internet, pre-satellite, relatively clean oceans, large tracts of forest, just a touch of global warming, no mass migrations, no intrusions by the other, and a world population of two and a half billion.

But that is not reality. Our oceans are filthy; information of all kinds, the scientific truth and the most ridiculous lies, are being disseminated at the speed of light; our forests are being decimated by man, by disease and by fire; the population of the world is a coal burning seven billion, a decreasing percentage actually understand how our tools work, and more and more mass migrations will occur as each piece of unfortunate land becomes uninhabitable. A wall on the southern border won't change this. Nor will a "Space Force".

Just when we need our leaders to look reality in the face, to acknowledge the world as it really is, and to get together to formulate a plan to control the population, to feed everybody, to spread the wealth a little more evenly, to decrease carbon emissions, save the oceans and forests, to use our scientific knowledge for good, to learn to live as a global community, we get Trump.

171

God (if you will pardon my use of an anachronistic idiom) help us all.

172

Trump, Dr Ford, and A Warning to Americans Session 82

October 8, 2018

I wrote a blog before the 2016 election of Donald Trump titled "the mental and emotional age of Donald Trump". I looked at a range of his behaviours and his speech patterns and considered the age at which such a behaviour would be typical for a boy or man, though not exemplary, not necessarily good, maybe even requiring some parental admonition, just typical. I arrived at an average of 14. Though some Trump statements required a pre-teen brain and some rose at least to 18 year-old jock talk.

A comment someone left on that blog was that I was being generous; it would have to be a particularly entitled and narcissistic 14 year-old.

More recently I listened to Trump mock the testimony of Dr. Ford and then go on about the threat the #MeToo movement poses for fine young men. He took on the voice of a boy talking to his mother about all the hard work he's done, about being offered a great job, but all this is over because some woman he's never even met is accusing him of things he's never done. How terrible this is for men and boys.

I might run across a small group of 14 year old boys with one of them going on in this vein, and two might be laughing, though more at the outrageous display of disregard for propriety than the content itself; another two would be cringing, but unable to break the code of teenage boys to never be a "pussy".

So the comment was fair. Only a nasty, narcissistic, and probably guilty 14 year-old could talk the way Trump so often talks.

Donald may be but a symptom of some other struggle in your country, my American friends, and I know you have some wide divides that need major bridgework, but he is doing damage to your country, more and more damage each day he has a voice.

They **were** laughing at him at the U.N. Much of the world is appalled

173

by him and all he represents. He throws oil on your fires; he cozies up to nasty dictators; he is stripping the USA of any moral high ground it ever might have had; he is creating fizzures in your country it may take decades to repair. He has reduced political discourse to a schoolyard brawl and international relations to flea market bartering.

He represents you, my friends, and how we see him we will begin to view you. We don't care how you see us, you may say, we are better than that. But there is a bit of psychology here you might not like. For gradually, whatever traits we assign to you, you will absorb, you will become.

This midterm you can show the world you are not all Trumpets; you can clip his wings and put him in a tail spin. Please do so.

Conrad Black and Donald Trump Session 83

October 12, 2018

I made the mistake of reading an article by Conrad Black. I usually avoid reading Lord Black of Crossharbour ("on leave") for I find his over-use of penultimate, supercilious, pretentious, swank, grandiloquent, Miltonian, show-offy adjectives very annoying.

But I did read his paean to Donald Trump, and then went for a bicycle ride to clear my head. But what should one expect from a man who gave up his Canadian citizenship for a Peerage in the UK, and once flew across the Atlantic to attend a costume party dressed as Cardinal Richelieu?

He refers to all immigrants entering the US through the border with Mexico as illiterate peasants and he thinks Donald Trump is the leader America needs. He does find Trump "grating" and that he takes "liberties with the truth", but he thinks that Trump can make America Great Again, and by that I think he is referring to a degree of respect we all must show for the man holding the true weapons of mass destruction in his hand. And by "respect" I think he means fear. Donald does seem to be on track for making America a country we soon will all fear.

Of course, Conrad Black, as a man barred from entering the United States, may simply be, like so many others, currying favour with the one man who could and might pardon him.

And then I read another by Lord Black along the same lines but more of a dissection of the geopolitical game afoot. And I was reminded of an experience from 1964. Bear with me for a moment.

Our first year medical school class went on a weekend retreat with faculty. This entailed a 90 minute bus ride to a resort north of Vancouver. By chance I sat next to our Professor of Physiology. The Vietnam war raged and was about to expand. My companion on that trip had fled McCarthy era USA rather than testify against his colleagues, who might or might not have attended a communist party meeting. So we talked Vietnam.

175

I was 24 at the time, but worldly and cynical. I argued geopolitics along the lines that it was better for the two major superpowers, the two competing ideologies, to be squaring off in the jungles of Vietnam rather than in the skies over Moscow and New York. He disagreed. It was simpler than that for my professor, who must have been in his 40's or 50's at the time. For him it was simply immoral. It was immoral for Americans to take their guns, their napalm, their warships and their helicopters to Vietnam and kill people. It was simply wrong.

By the end of that trip I had concluded that if he could remain idealistic in his 50's, surely cynicism in my 20's was, at least, premature. It wasn't long after that I found myself in a placard carrying crowd in front of the American Consulate chanting: "Hey, Hey, LBJ, how many kids did you kill today?"

But why I was reminded of this was because Conrad Black was writing with his usual elegance and erudition about the geopolitics of recent years, the new balance of power, the symbolic chess game played by nation states, and prognosticating about the geopolitics of the future. And it is this examination of geopolitics that I can hear from other politicians, commentators, advisors, other writers. And it reminds me of my self, age 24, arguing, albeit more naively, about these world events and shifts and movements and power struggles as if they are being played on large chessboards by giants, with the pawns and rooks representing a few million to a billion people. And talking about it and playing the game as if they experience, think about, Joseph Stalin's famous observation as advice, rather than the cynical observation of a sociopath. "One man's death is a tragedy; the death of millions is a statistic".

My medical school professor could see beyond the geopolitics and the million death statistic to the terrified little girl fleeing the sticky horror of napalm.

The Bannons, Boltons, Millers, Trumps and Conrad Blacks of this world do not, cannot.

I do not want them to have any influence over myself or the lives of my children and grandchildren. We need to stop listening to them and focus instead on the little girl fleeing the napalm and the kid from Honduras locked in an American cage.

176

Interesting Times
Session 84

October 22, 2018

"May you live in interesting times." is an old Chinese curse that places an interesting twist on the word interesting.

And these be they I think. And not just because the world's most powerful nation has the world's dumbest president, not because the digital revolution allows me to write this and send it to your phones, tablets and computers, and not because a space station orbits up above us, and not because we now understand there is really no "up" within our space time continuum and expanding universe.

But because the generations alive today can be consciously aware of both the beginning and end of our existence. And by beginning I mean the enlightenment, the industrial revolution, and the birth of science, public health and medicine, and by "end" I mean the ravages of global warming and nuclear conflagration.

My generation had grandparents who moved from horse drawn buggies to motor cars, and they had grandparents of their own who left the farms and migrated to the cities for jobs in the new factories.

Up until then the human population was rather stable, despite pestilence, tribal and religious wars, famine and hardship. For thousands of years and thousands of migrations the ecosystem sustained, and life went on. Short and brutal though it was for most. And then suddenly (a mere blink in the life of our galaxy) we find we have 7 billion people on earth, insufficient forests to absorb the carbon we emit, all 7 billion gasping for breath on a wee polluted globe with a rising temperature.

I now have grandchildren who will experience the true disasters of global warming and over population, and they may have children and grandchildren who will witness the end of times.

From start to finish a mere 10 generations or so. And we, I think, live within that unique middle space of being able to imagine, experience, hear about and read about the beginning, and being able to see and imagine the inexorable movement toward the end. Interesting times indeed.

Unless we somehow control population growth, ease it back to a sustainable 4 or 5 billion, find a way of reducing and absorbing carbon, and sweep Donald Trump into the dustbin of history.

But, speaking of Donald, I must check out those Cohen tapes about the payoffs to Stormy and that other playmate.

Fear and Loathing from Washington Session 85

October 24, 2018

Some years ago driving from New Orleans to Ontario I was cruising through the bucolic landscape of Kentucky when a talk radio show asked callers about guns. The first caller suggested buying many guns before the government undermined the second amendment. The second caller disagreed. It was ammunition they needed to buy before the government controlled the amount one could purchase. That's what they would control, he asserted, not guns. And he was ready with his multiple guns and his great store of ammunition. He would be armed and ready on his roof top when those "terr'rists come over the hills."

It wasn't the American obsession with guns that struck me so much as the fear and insecurity. I tried to imagine a full company of Islamic terrorists crawling through the blue grass and over the rolling hills of Kentucky. Fear, insecurity, and a total lack of perspective.

More recently I watched some white suburban American women being interviewed. I think three were leaning toward the democrats in this coming midterm, while at least one was a Trump supporter. This was shortly after his "Horseface" comment. When asked why she supported Trump and by extension the Republicans, this woman's answer was simple and heart felt: "He has kept us safe." She didn't say safe from what. Islamic terrorists, hordes of illegal immigrants, North Korean missiles, socialism?

Though I have compared Donald Trump's brain to that of the less-than-average 14 year-old, there is some evil genius in this mix. Fear, insecurity, and a lack of perspective, perspectives of time, history, impact, and size. These are the characteristics of a population ready to give up on democracy and welcome a tyrant, and Donald Trump is feeding these insecurities on a Paleo diet.

A caravan of Hondurans approaches from the south, and Trump hypes them into a plague of biblical proportions and threatens to send

179

troops to close the border. If you stand in the middle of them, he says, and look around you will see "Middle Easterns" and criminals. Asked for proof of this he boldly says, "There is no proof of anything." – an ironic admission that he can say and proclaim whatever comes to his mind.

And then he says he is withdrawing from the nuclear arms control deal with Russia.

Now he is scaring me.

So the democrats need to develop some effective counter punching, rather than the platitudes I've been hearing. Here are a few:

"Only a horse's ass would call a woman a horseface."

"A few hundred or even a few thousand women, children and men from Honduras are not a threat to the American Way of Life. But putting troops on the border and children in cages is."

"For God's sake, any control over nuclear proliferation is better than none."

"Stop dismantling the international agreements that have kept the world from total destruction since 1945."

"Your anxieties are misplaced. It is not a few Hondurans that will destroy the US of A but climate change, income inequality, racism, isolationism, criminalization of the poor and mentally ill, and unwarranted trust in the Plutocracy of Donald Trump."

The Culpability of a President Session 86

October 29, 2018

There are always men around, men from age 18 to 70, who are capable of committing hate crimes. These are boys and men who always blame others for their failures, infirmities, losses, inadequacies, and perceived slights. They harbour resentments. Their thinking is delusional or just this side of delusional. They may fantasize revenge, the settling of scores, the righting of wrongs. This particular disorder of personality will usually preclude successful intimate relationships, long term employment and even good friends – the very antidotes to distorted and paranoid thinking.

Isolated it festers, grows and deepens. "They are to blame."

But usually such men don't act on their convictions, their fantasies. At least they don't act on them without some kind of encouragement, support, and sanction.

Unfortunately such encouragement is now readily available on internet sites. This was probably the source of encouragement that set the man off to driving his van into pedestrians (women) on Yonge street.

But for the man who sent pipe bombs in the mail last week, his move from anger, conspiracy theory and threats to action, the encouragement undoubtedly came from the President of the United States. In fact the word "sanction" fits in this case because the encouragement came from authority.

The call has been to "tone down the rhetoric". That is too weak. Men and women in power need to know their words can foster peace and cooperation or they can incite violence. There are always some men who are waiting for just such encouragement, just such permission.

Donald Trump is not personally and specifically responsible for those pipe bombs, but he is culpable.

He needn't "tone down the rhetoric", he needs to "stop inciting violence".

As I was writing this another delusional man committed multiple murders in a synagogue. His encouragement to act on his antisemitic delusion seems to have come from a social media site called Gab and alt-right conspiracy theorists, but the caravan of "invaders" moving through Mexico may have been the final trigger, and we all know how much Trump has hyped that fear, and, for that matter, threatened to send in a platoon of men with guns. "Screw the optics," wrote this killer, "I'm going in."

Trump's remedy for this was more guns, armed security within houses of worship, before he was distracted by a baseball game and tweeting out a criticism of the manager for pulling the successful pitcher in the last innings of the game.

Nero came to mind.

Trump Trashes the Veneer of Civilization Session 87

October 31, 2018

Just as we humans always overestimate our memories and find ourselves regretting we didn't commit to paper or snapshot yesterday or last week, we also overestimate the extent to which our actions are guided by thoughtful consideration and choice.

We are easily influenced, especially if the influence is playing to our rat brain, to centuries of old survival coding.

The crowd of ordinary people chant in unison, "Lock her up. Lock her up." It is, of course, entirely irrational, a bit nasty, and quite contrary to all due processes of judgment and punishment that have developed within western civilization over the past 100 years. I scan the part of the crowd shown on my monitor and I can't find one person who has chosen not to chant.

But then we already know this about humans within crowds and mobs and humans under the influence of a charismatic authority, even when that authority is self-proclaimed. It is a small percent that can resist at that moment, that can buck the trend, be contrary, who can ask themselves, "Is this right?"

We know this from history. We know this from the Nuremberg Trials, from human behaviour in times of armed conflict and occupation. And we know this from some simple experiments in social psychology.

And we also know that among us are a few who respond eagerly to license and sanction, the go ahead to unleash the beast within, to act on a simmering hatred. Again we know this from history and contemporary observation.

Though the assumption of free will and personal responsibility is a cornerstone of human society, it does not negate the reality of what is written above.

We know these things about human behaviour. All our leaders should know these things.

So, yes, when Donald Trump's crowds chant "Lock her up." and "CNN sucks." and when he tells his people they should fear the caravan of "invaders", and when he fails to condemn the Alt-right extremists or other tyrants, **he is culpable**

To US Citizens – Tuesday is Your Last Chance Session 88

November 5, 2018

There must have been a moment, a day, sometime between 1927 and 1939 when it became too late to alter the course of world affairs as one Adolf Hitler rose to power and brought about the destruction of Europe.

The Austrian National Socialist party won only 779 votes in all of Austria in the general election of 1927. But their membership doubled each year after that and by the early 30's one of their slogans was, "500,000 unemployed – 400,000 Jews – Simple way out; vote National Socialist".

Historians can trace the seeds of WWII to WWI, but still there must have been a day when it was too late to stop WWII and the holocaust. Perhaps that day was the last opportunity to **not** vote for the National Socialists. Should not the slogan in the preceding paragraph been enough of a warning? Is not the code in "Simple way out" obvious? Or the juxtaposition of 500,000 unemployed to 400,000 Jews?

Apparently not.

I am writing this because I fear this Tuesday, the 6th of November, 2018, is the last day Americans can go to the polls and change the course of history.

I listened to some Trump supporters last night and I find they are just as deaf to the implications of the words of Donald Trump as the citizens of Europe were to that slogan:

"500,000 unemployed – 400,000 Jews – Simple way out; vote National Socialist".

"I tell the truth when I can," says Trump, without a flicker of irony. "Consider rocks as rifles if migrants throw them". "...very bad thugs and gang members and middle 'easterns'..", "rapists and murderers..", "Invaders".

Trump uses simpler code than the Nazi's of the early 30's. It should

185

be easy to decipher, and then to grasp the full implications, and then to recoil from them.

Tuesday, November 6, 2018 may be that last day, my American friends, when you can stop this malignant rush to tribal warfare and the destruction of democracy.

Vote.

A Cornered Narcissist is not a Pretty Sight
Session 88

November 19, 2018

Here is what to expect:

Increasing displays of petulance, irrational accusations, self-pity, rage, and depression, while he continues to seek out adoring crowds and fawning world leaders wherever he can find them.

This depression will take the form of blunt affect, self-imposed isolation, and paranoia.

I was struck by Trump's demeanour right after the midterms. The news channels referred to it as upbeat, positive. His words (the actual words) started out upbeat, declaring the midterms a Republican "victory", calling it "great", before taking pot shots at all his favourite enemies and hinting at a democratic/deep state conspiracy against him, but his affect throughout this was flat, his pronunciation dull, his face blunted. even when using the words "great" and "victory" – at least until his petulant rage at Jim Acosta.

With the democrats now having the majority in the House, the republicans weakened in many State legislatures, the firing of Jeff Sessions, we are now into the endgame.

I don't profess to feel any certainty how this will unfold. The possibilities include everything from impeachment to endless investigations to a thin gruel of feigned bipartisanship to more unrest, polarization, and violence.

But Donald Trump's responses are predictable, and highly visible in his five tweets today attacking the press and the Mueller Investigation with even more recklessness and less attention to reality than we have seen before.

There was a time when a mad king could be isolated and the kingdom protected from his madness. Unfortunately we now have twitter and more than a few sycophants surrounding this president.

And many more commentators still trying to shine a kind light on his outrageous words and notions.

Perhaps the world's frightening march back to 1913 with the rise of nationalism, the erection of fences, the dissolution of agreements, and the rebirth of oligarchs will proceed without Trump. Or, or, or America might return to an improved version of itself as the beacon of successful liberal democracy, perhaps even with universal health care, gun control, less racism and a major role to play addressing climate change. I hope they try. Whatever poison flows below the 49th parallel tends to seep into Canada.

So, my American friends, it is now time for damage control and careful planning. If only you could promise him a statue bigger than Lincoln's and the rating of "best president ever" in the history books in return for his retirement to Mar-a-Lago, quietly and permanently.

Dumb as a Rock Session 89

December 12, 2018

Having lost the centrality and privilege of childhood and now struggling with their own insecurities there is a moment some teens decide, and announce to me, that ALL their peers are stupid, dumb as rocks, and lying. Usually for teens trapped in this moment of narcissistic injury they make one exception. For boys it may be an online friend supporting his complaints in a gaming forum, for girls it is a best friend who goes to a different school.

Usually they grow past this period of developmental disappointment: A combination of time, some success at something, some judicious counselling, the love of a parent, finding a boyfriend or girlfriend, and sometimes taking the right medication for excess anxiety.

The analogy with Donald J. Trump is imperfect. For the teenagers their "dumb as rocks" peers comprise a classroom of 30 or a school of 1000. It is the limit of their experience at this age. New acceptable friends are hard to find.

But Donald, for every friend, associate and peer he decides is "dumb as a rock" there are two new friends waiting in the wings for a role in the play, and a chance to be best of buddies.

But the language he uses is the same:the playground accusations, the remarkable hyperbole, the name calling, the self reference, the projections, and the underlying insecurities.

I suspect the only reason Donald's tweets sometimes sound more sophisticated than a 15 year old complaining to me is that he is quoting some words and numbers from Fox & Friends, as in "the 245 times James Comey told the investigators he didn't know.".

As this drama unfolds over the next few months I hope the adults in the room remember we are dealing with a very narcissistic 14 year old with the moral compass of a peanut.

Perhaps we can resurrect Donald's parents and have Mueller and Congress hand the whole thing off to family court.

David Laing Dawson

We explore and investigate our world and ourselves through science and through art. With science we define reality, its dimensions, its limitations, its probabilities. With art we seek revelation, a truth beyond the surface, and a glimpse of that which science cannot define.

I am a physician and an artist. The physician prevents me from pursuing art as mere entertainment, as excess, as egomania, though that would be fun. The artist prevents me from believing I can rely on science and received wisdom, though that would be comforting.

But the one always informs the other.

As Victor Hugo put it: "..science is a ladder...poetry is winged flight."

Printed in the USA
CPSIA information can be obtained
at www.ICGtesting.com
LVHW041359260824
789277LV00009B/211

9 781927 6373